DATING

Guidelines from the Bible

SCOTT KIRBY

BAKER BOOK HOUSE
Grand Rapids, Michigan

First printing, July 1979
Second printing, September 1979
Third printing, April 1980
Fourth printing, December 1980
Fifth printing, May 1981
Sixth printing, September 1981
Seventh printing, January 1982
Eighth printing, April 1982

Printed in the United States of America

Unless otherwise noted, all Scripture references are taken from the New American Standard Bible, copyright 1960, 1962, 1963, 1968, 1971, 1972, 1973, 1975 by the Lockman Foundation, La Habra, California. Used by permission.

This study on dating, though revised for publication, was originally submitted as a seminary thesis project. It is published with permission from Dallas Theological Seminary.

Dedication

This book is dedicated to my precious wife, Rhonda, who was such an encouragement and help while I wrote it. It is also dedicated to my parents, Ben and Jane Kirby, who instilled so many of these moral values in me at an early age.

Acknowledgments

I want to thank Dr. Paul Meier, Dr. Warren Benson, and Mr. Woody Williams for their valuable guidance and encouragement.

I also want to thank the many young people who have participated in my dating seminars and have enthusiastically given advice and input.

Contents

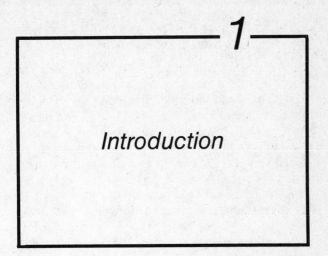

Introduction

Perhaps the greatest problems that Christian young people face today are in their dating and love life. Several years of youth work have convinced me of the great need for sound biblical teaching in the area of love, sex, and dating. Often I have seen wrong dating habits spiritually destroy young people who were beginning to show an interest in spiritual things.

The average young person is very interested in love and dating. Yet most of them experience great frustration, discouragement, and depression in this aspect of their life. Some are discouraged because they are struggling with sexual temptation in their dating relationships. Others are depressed because their dating life is a "big zero." Still others are discouraged because they like a special person who does not seem even to know that they exist.

Tragically, young Christians are exposed to almost no good biblical teaching in this area. But they are almost constantly fed a steady secular diet of misinformation about love, sex, and dating. Television, radio, movies, billboards, magazines, books, and a multitude of other sources all preach the gospel of sexual liberation to the young believer. If you are a young single, what are you to do in the face of all this? The purpose of this book on Christian dating is to provide some answers. In Proverbs 12:25, we read, "Anxiety in the heart of a man weighs it down, but a good word makes it glad." It is hoped that this book on dating will give a "good word" to the hearts of those young Christians who are anxiously weighed down by problems in the area of dating and love.

What Is "Dating"?

Perhaps the best place to start in a book on dating is to define at the very beginning what we mean by "dating." When we talk of dating we are not so much talking about "a date" as we are about a relationship between a guy and a girl.

Dating can be better understood if it is looked at in the context of all opposite-sex relationships. Below is a diagram which illustrates the four levels of opposite-sex relationships. Each level is based upon the level beneath it and is vitally dependent on success in the lower level. The better one succeeds in the lower levels, the better he will succeed in the next level. For instance, the first and primary relationship is *friendship*. But notice that dating is based upon friendship. The better one is at developing good friendships the better chances he has for success in dating relationships. If you want to begin preparing yourself for good dating relationships, then begin focusing on developing good friendships.

The second level of opposite-sex relationships is *dating*. Notice that there are three kinds of dating relationships—casual dates, special dates, and steady dates. Casual dates are "take it or leave it dates." You have no special emotional involvement with that person. Girls, perhaps a guy calls you up to

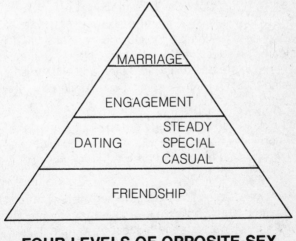

FOUR LEVELS OF OPPOSITE-SEX RELATIONSHIPS

go play tennis. You don't really care much about the guy but you go out with him just to get out of the house and have something to do. With a special date, you have some emotional involvement. Girls, perhaps a really great guy that you've had your eye on calls you up on a Wednesday night. You feel a tingle of excitement in your stomach when you realize who is calling. He talks a while and then asks you out for Saturday night. You play it cool and say, "Just a second, let me go check my calendar." (Pause.) "Uh, I think I'm free then. Yes, I'd enjoy going out Saturday night." You small talk a few more minutes and then as soon as he hangs up you call twenty of your friends to tell them the news. The rest of the week passes very slowly as you long for Saturday to come. Finally, the Big Day arrives. You begin at ten o'clock Saturday morning taking a bath, doing your hair, fixing your nails, deciding what to wear, and putting on makeup. Now *that's* what I mean by a special date! Of course, steady dating is when you are committed to dating only one special person and he or she is committed to dating only you (as far as you know!).

After dating comes *engagement.* Engagement is the period before marriage when two people commit themselves to marry and are preparing toward that marriage.

Marriage often follows engagement. I say "often" because 40 to 50 percent of all engagements are broken.[1] Marriage is the highest of all human rela-

---

1. Henry Bowman, *Marriage for Moderns,* McGraw Hill, p. 144.

tionships and is highly encouraged in Scripture, as we shall see later.

The Bible Is Our Textbook

Much has been written on dating. Almost all high school and college marriage and family living textbooks have chapters on dating and love. But different books have different perspectives, and they do not teach morals. Teachers of marriage and family living classes today simply try to help the student "clarify" the moral standards and values he already holds.

How then can we know what is right and what is wrong? Is there nothing by which we can guide our lives? Thank goodness there is! God has given His Word, and that Word is found in the Bible. The Bible is our road map for successful living in tough times. Some people think that the Bible is simply a sweet book of meditations. But the Bible is much more than that. Paul writes in II Timothy 3:16 that "all Scripture is inspired by God [literally, God-breathed] and profitable for teaching, for reproof, for correction, for training in righteousness; that the man [and woman] of God may be adequate, equipped for every good work [i.e., able to meet every situation that life offers.]"

In this book on dating the Bible is our primary and final source of authority. Our main concern will be to see what God has to say about this matter. We must realize, however, that *the Bible has absolutely nothing specific to say about dating!* We don't read about the courtship days of Mary and Joseph in the Bible. Nowhere in the Bible is dating mentioned even once.

The reason for this is that in Bible times couples did not date as we do today. Dating is a cultural thing, and it is not practiced in many parts of the world, even today. Back in Bible times, marriages were arranged by parents, and young people married very early. Mary was probably only thirteen or fourteen when she became engaged to Joseph and was perhaps only fourteen or fifteen when she gave birth to Jesus.

Though the Bible doesn't have anything to say specifically about dating, it does have a lot to say about the use and misuse of sex, the marriage relationship, and relationships between people in general. Therefore, we will draw *principles* from these things and apply them to dating.

Attitude Is Important

Before we begin to discuss dating I think it is very important that we first examine our hearts and attitudes. As Paul says in II Corinthians 5:9, "we have as our ambition . . . to be pleasing to Him [God]." Paul's passion and ambition in life was to please the Lord—in everything! And unless your ambition and heart's desire is to please the Lord in your dating life, reading this book will be a waste of time. Do you really want Jesus to put His stamp of approval upon your dating relationships? Do you want Him to be pleased with your motive for dating? Do you want Him to be pleased with your actions on dates? Do you want Him to be pleased with your choice of dates? The desire to please the Lord is vital and foundational to the whole issue of Christian dating. Let me encourage you right now, before you read on, to bow your head and tell God that you want Him to be fully pleased with your dating life. And then tell Him that you are willing to make any changes in your dating life that He shows you as you read this book.

In the Beginning . . .

Beginning in the Book of Beginnings

The best place to start a study of Christian dating is at the *beginning,* of course. And so we will turn to the Book of Genesis. Genesis is the first book in the Bible; in fact, the word *genesis* literally means "beginnings." In Genesis 2:18-25 we discover four very important things from this book of beginnings that will give us a foundation for everything else we say about Christian dating.

It Is Not Good for Man To Be Alone

In Genesis 1, God created the light and said that it was good. Then He created the dry lands and the seas and said that they also were good. Next He created all the vegetation and said that it too was good. Then He created all the living creatures, including man, and even said that they were good. But then, in Genesis 2:18, God said *for the first time* that something was not good. God said, "It is not good for the man to be alone; I will make him a helper suitable for him."

It is not good for man to be alone. I remember in my early high school days that I was ashamed of being attracted to girls. And adults didn't help this by their constant kidding! As I grew older, however, I discovered that being attracted to the opposite sex is nothing to be ashamed of and certainly is not unusual. The important thing to remember is that God created us this way. Back in the Garden of Eden, God made man with a woman-sized void in his life. And God created woman with a man-sized void in her life. This attraction between the sexes is therefore perfectly natural and healthy.

God saw that the best solution to man's loneliness was "a helper suitable for him." The word *helper* describes a person who comes to the aid of someone in need. The phrase *suitable for him* literally means "corresponding to him." The idea then is that God planned to give man someone who completes and complements him. Only man and woman together make a whole. Separated, there is a sense of incompleteness.

When I first studied this passage in Genesis I discovered something very strange. You would think that when God saw that man needed a mate He would make him one immediately, right? Wrong! Instead, God started bringing all the animals to Adam and told Adam to begin naming them. Why? I think that God meant to show Adam his need for a mate. God knew that Adam was lonely and needed a helper, but Adam didn't know this. How could he know that he needed a woman? He had never even seen one! God decided to show Adam his need by showing him all the animals. As Adam was naming the animals, it must have dawned upon him that they all had mates. There were two of each kind, similar, and yet separate. And so, (and I am speculating!) I think Adam started looking for his mate. As he was anxiously peering into the forest, wondering if his mate would be the next to come out, a pair of hippopotamuses came out. "No, Lord, that's not exactly what I'm looking for." Then came out a pair of gorillas. "Lord, that's closer, but she's awfully hairy!" And so, though Adam kept looking, unfortunately no mate came out of the woods. We read in verse 20 that "the man gave names to all the cattle, and to the birds of the sky, and to every beast of the field, but for Adam there was not found a helper suitable for him."

God Made Woman from Man

God's solution to man's loneliness was to make woman. The Bible says that God caused a deep sleep to fall on Adam, when God performed surgery and removed a rib from Adam's side. God then formed that rib into a woman. Adam traded a rib for a wife and I'm sure never regretted the trade. Over four hundred years ago Matthew Henry wrote concerning this passage, "She was not made of his head to top him; nor out of his feet to be trampled upon by him; but out of his side to be equal with him, under his arm, to be protected, and near to his heart, to be loved."[1]

It says in verse 22 that when God made woman from man's rib He "fashioned" that rib into a woman. The word *fashion* literally means "to build." The same word is used to describe King Solomon building the temple. Woman is the highest expression of God's creative handiwork, and she was fashioned especially for man. God fashioned every curve of her body in order that she might please and satisfy man.

God Brought the Woman to the Man

The Bible says that after God created the woman, He brought her to the man. According to Genesis 2:23, man's response was, "This is now bone of my bones, and flesh of my flesh; she shall be called Woman, because she was taken out of Man." These words sound matter-of-fact, but many commentators acknowledge that the original Hebrew reveals a sense of excitement on Adam's part.

I once heard someone say that just as God brought Adam's mate to him when he was asleep in the will of God, so God will bring our mate to us when we are asleep in the will of God. We'll talk about this more later, but there is some truth in this concept. God was fully aware of Adam's need and was working in His own time and plan to perfectly fulfill that need. In the

1. Matthew Henry, *A Commentary on the Whole Bible*, 6 vols. (Old Tappan, N. J.: Revell, n. d.), 1:20.

same way, God is aware of our need and is working according to His will and time to provide for that need.

God Created Sex

In Genesis 2:24 we read, "For this cause a man shall leave his father and his mother, and shall cleave to his wife; and they shall become one flesh." Here the Bible reveals that God created sex and put His blessing on it. Notice that God created sex *before* Adam's and Eve's sin and fall, as recorded in Genesis 3. God created sex and it is good! I want you to see right here at the start that God is very positive toward sex. Unfortunately, many people think that God has put a hex on sex! But God is not down on sex. It is true that God is down on the misuse of sex, but sex in the right relationship is part of His perfect will.

But what is the "right relationship" for sex? God says that the only right place for sex is in the marriage relationship (cf. Gen. 2:24, Heb. 13:4, I Cor. 7:1,2). Notice in Genesis 2:24 that leaving comes before cleaving. Marriage comes before sex. Sex is good and right, but only at the right time, in the right relationship, with the right person—within the marriage relationship. Otherwise, it is sin.

Why Date?

We should never do anything without a purpose. Life is far too short to waste it in meaningless activities. Someone once said: "If you aim at nothing, you will hit it every time." In other words, our purpose determines our actions. I think we ought to have a purpose for dating. We shouldn't date simply in order to have something to do or because all our friends are dating. I think it is important that we all think through our reasons for dating. As I've considered this issue myself, I've come up with a list of five primary purposes for dating. Perhaps you can add to this list, but I think that it covers the main reasons for dating.

To Grow Socially, Emotionally, and Spiritually

Proverbs 27:17 says that as "iron sharpens iron, so one man sharpens another." Each of us has special needs and rough edges in our lives that need to be worked on and smoothed out. In a Christ-centered dating relationship we can discover our strengths and weaknesses and discern areas of our lives that need to be worked on. A dating relationship gives us an opportunity to learn how to better relate to others and to polish our social and communication skills.

I also believe that it is God's will that we grow spiritually as the result of a dating relationship. I think God's ideal is that as you get closer to the person you are dating, you also get closer to God. The relationship should cause you to have a greater desire to pray, to get into the Word, and to share Christ with others. A dating relationship helps us grow either toward God or away from God.

To Learn How To Better Communicate with the Opposite Sex

Real communication is an art that must be learned. It is easy to talk on a superficial level, but it is very difficult to really learn to open up your heart to another person, to share how you "really feel." I think dating is an opportunity to learn how to open up your soul to another person. Try it. It's difficult, but well worth it.

It is tragic to see so many couples who can't talk to one another. The only way they can express themselves to one another is physically. The physical relationship is all they have in common. Needless to say, this is a very *shallow* relationship.

To Help Fulfill the Need To Love and To Be Loved

Perhaps the most basic need that man has beside the essential biological needs of food and water is the need to love and to be loved. Dating is a relationship where we can learn to give and to receive love. We need to realize, however, that God can fulfill these needs in many other ways apart from a dating or marriage relationship.

To Have a Good Time and To Relax

It is easy to make dating so "spiritual" that it is no longer any fun. Dating should be a good time! Everyone needs to relax, let loose, and play. All work and no play makes us unbalanced. Dating is a great opportunity just to have a good time with someone you care about.

To Help Shape an Ideal Image of Our Future Mate and Bring Us into Contact with Potential Marriage Partners

We usually marry someone we have dated. That isn't very profound, but it's true. As we date, we begin to subconsciously decide what we want in a future mate. Paul Meier, a Christian psychiatrist, suggests that "a person should date as many members of the opposite sex as possible in order to evaluate what type of mate would suit him best."[2]

Conclusion

The whole point of this chapter is that dating is a good thing and that young people should seek healthy dating relationships. Some people feel that dating is not a good idea because of the many problems that can arise out of dating relationships. True, there are many problems associated with dating, such as breakups and impure physical relationships, but the advantages of dating *far outweigh* the disadvantages.

We have seen that way back in the Garden of Eden God designed men and women to be attracted to one another and to need relationships with one another. We have also seen the benefits of dating. Dating helps us to grow both emotionally and spiritually. It teaches us to communicate. It helps to fulfill the need to love and to be loved. It gives us an opportunity to relax and to have a good time. Also, it helps us to shape an ideal image of a future mate and brings us into contact with potential marriage partners.

For these reasons, I hope you have a positive attitude about dating. I suggest that you bow your

2. Paul D. Meier, *Christian Child-Rearing and Personality Development,* p. 191.

head right now and ask God to give you an opportunity in a God-honoring dating relationship to practice the principles that you learn in this book.

Discussion Questions

1. In Genesis 2:18, why do you think God said that it is not good for man to be alone?

2. What does God mean by "a helper suitable for him" (v. 18)?

3. Why does the writer of Genesis suddenly switch from Adam's need in verse 18 to naming the animals in vv. 19–20 and then back to Adam's need in v. 21?

4. In v. 21, what is the significance of woman being formed out of the rib of man? (see I Cor. 11:3, 8–12).

5. What do you think Adam means in v. 23 when he says, "This is now bone of my bones, and flesh of my flesh?"

6. Contrast Genesis 2:25 with 3:7, 10, 11. What do these passages teach about the marriage relationship?

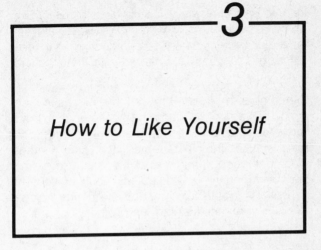

3

How to Like Yourself

Do you really like yourself the way you are? Do you feel good about yourself? Or do you want to change some major things about your appearance and personality?

The average young person is very dissatisfied with his appearance and personality. He is either too tall or too short, too fat or too thin, too light or too dark. His ears are too big, he has acne, a crooked nose, bad teeth, bad eyes, a high voice, a speech impediment, or a thousand other defects.

Some time ago I taught about ninety young people at a retreat. I gave them a survey to determine how they felt about themselves and discovered the following results: Thirty-three said that they often felt ugly;

17

thirteen said that they sometimes felt that others would be better off if they were dead; twelve said that they didn't like themselves; eight said that they sometimes felt that God made a mistake in making them.

I remember that I hated myself when I was in high school. I was skinny, had a bad case of acne, had bad eyes, and had a speech impediment. This made me very insecure, so I retreated into a shell. I imagined that people laughed at me because of my speech impediment. So I kept my mouth closed. As a result, I was antisocial and had few friends. I didn't like myself and neither did many others like me.

Self-Love

This personal illustration introduces an important concept. Before you can love others, you must first love yourself. By the same token, you must first like yourself before others will like you.

This concept is clearly seen in the Bible. Jesus said that we should love our neighbor *as ourselves* (Mark 12:31). Before you can genuinely love your neighbor, you must have a healthy self-love. Not a sick, boastful, arrogant pride, but a healthy, genuine good feeling about yourself.

In the Book of Ephesians, the apostle Paul exhorts husbands to "love their own wives as their own bodies" (5:28). Paul assumes that before a man can really love his wife, he has to first have a good feeling about himself and his own body.

This concept of first loving yourself before you can really love others is basic to a healthy and successful dating life. Christian psychiatrist Paul Meier writes, "A person who doesn't love himself in a healthy way will find it impossible to develop genuine love relationships with others."[1] Unless you feel good about yourself, unless you like yourself, you won't have the confidence to be yourself and to let the barriers down when you're around the opposite sex. You'll feel self-conscious and uncomfortable.

Self-confidence is one of the keys to a successful dating life, and the key to self-confidence is liking yourself. Many young people have come to me and complained that they don't know how to talk to the opposite sex. They don't know what to say. The solution is found in building self-confidence. And this confidence comes through developing a healthy self-image.

Building a Healthy Self-Image

You Are an Important Person To God

Sometimes we feel that we are unloved and useless. But even though we may feel that we are unimportant, God feels that we are very important. The Bible teaches that we are made in the image of God (Gen. 1:26). The Bible also teaches that if we are Christians we are children of God (John 1:12; Rom. 8:14). God

1. Paul Meier, *Christian Child-Rearing and Personality Development*, p. 26.

is our Father, and He loves us and cares for us with a father's love. Also, as Christians, we are worth a great deal to God, for our salvation was purchased by the precious blood of His son (I Peter 1:18, 19). Jesus Christ died for you. He wouldn't have died for you if you weren't important to Him. Even if no one else in the whole world cares for you, God does. Others may call you a nobody, but God calls you a somebody!

God Is Far More Concerned with Inward Character than with Outward Appearances

We live in a society that programs us to think that external things like beauty, strength, clothes, academic achievement, and material possessions are most important. We measure a person's worth on the basis of these things. If you have these things, you're a somebody. If you don't have these things, then you're a nobody.

But society's message that external things are the most important things is a lie! God says that inward character is far more important than external characteristics. In I Samuel 16, God told Samuel to go to the house of Jesse to anoint the new king of Israel. God had told Samuel that His anointed one was one of the eight sons of Jesse, but He didn't tell Samuel which son it would be. When Samuel arrived at Jesse's house and looked at Jesse's eldest son, he was greatly impressed and thought to himself, "Surely the Lord's anointed is before Him" (v. 6). But then the Lord interrupted and said to Samuel, "Do not look at his appearance or at the height of his stature, because I have rejected him; for God sees not as man sees, for man looks at the outward appearance, but the Lord looks at the heart" (v. 7). This is a spiritual truth that we should never forget.

The people around you, your classmates at school, the television and radio media all glorify the outward appearance. They teach that the external things are the most important. But let us see what God says about outward appearance.

Beauty

The world says that physical beauty is the key to happiness. If you are beautiful, then you're a some-body. Advertisements on television and in maga-zines imply that physical attractiveness (beautiful hair, good complexion, white teeth, fresh breath) is necessary for succeeding in all areas of life.

The problem is that most of us are not exceptionally beautiful or handsome. Most of us are just average, and we are made to feel inferior because of that. In Proverbs 31:30, however, God puts this whole issue of beauty into perspective: "Charm is deceitful and beauty is vain, but a woman who fears the Lord, she shall be praised." Charm is "deceitful" because it leads us to think that a person who is outwardly charming must also be inwardly beautiful. But one has nothing to do with the other. Beauty is "vain" because it passes away so quickly. Physical beauty fades with each passing year. However, there is a type of beauty that does not diminish; in fact, it grows and deepens with time. It is the beauty of the soul that comes from walking with God. (I Peter 3:3–5). The key is not to focus so much on outward beauty, but to focus instead on developing inward beauty. The way to become a "somebody" is to concentrate on developing godly character and a close walk with the Lord. "The woman who fears the Lord, she shall be praised!" That's a promise from God.

Strength

At high schools and colleges the athlete is often the big man on campus. In the same way that women often focus on beauty, men usually focus on strength. In past generations, young people worshiped as heroes great military men, politicians, and explorers. But today, many idolize athletic heroes—especially professional athletes.

Participation in athletics is good in that it builds endurance, teamwork, and is good exercise, but it can become overemphasized. God shows us how to keep this in perspective, as Paul writes in I Timothy 4:7, 8: "Discipline yourself for the purpose of godliness; for bodily discipline is only little profit, but godliness is profitable for all things, since it holds promise for the present life and also for the life to come." Paul is saying that though bodily discipline is good, the discipline of the soul is far more important. Tragically, there are Christians who can discipline themselves to run two miles a day and yet can't discipline themselves to read two chapters of the Bible a day. Something is wrong when we spend hours a week participating in athletics and spend only minutes a week in prayer and Bible study.

The psalmist writes, "He [God] does not delight in the strength of the horse; He does not take pleasure in the legs of a man. The Lord favors those who fear Him, those who wait for His lovingkindness" (Ps. 147:10, 11). The world may glorify athletics and strength, and these things are good, but God is far more delighted in the man who loves and fears Him. Inward character is more important to God than outward strength.

Clothes

Clothes are a status symbol today, especially among students. People are preoccupied with wearing the "right" clothes in order to be accepted. Girls especially worry about clothes and what others will think about what they wear. Many of us have the idea that if we wear the right clothes people will like us.

We should, of course, try to dress neatly and attractively, but we ought to realize that clothing is not nearly as important as we make it out to be. Jesus said, "Why are you so anxious about clothing?" (Matt. 6:28). God is much more concerned about a person's heart than He is about his or her outward attire. The apostle Peter wrote to the women of his day, "Let not your adornment be external only— braiding the hair, and wearing gold jewelry, and putting on dresses; but let it be the hidden person of the heart, with the imperishable quality of a gentle and quiet spirit, which is precious in the sight of God. For in this way in former times the holy women also, who hoped in God, used to adorn themselves . . ." (I Peter 3:3–5).

Peter is not preaching against dressing attractively, but he is saying that the quality of your heart is much more important than the quality of your clothes. Dress yourself in godly character. Too many Christians on Sunday morning are more concerned about how they look to others than how they look to God. God looks at inward character, not outward dress.

Academic Achievement

Often students feel that they are failures in life if they don't get good grades in school. And parents, too, can give this false impression to their children. Tragically, in some families parental acceptance is based on good grades. School systems measure the intellectual ability of a person with grades. And too often students make these grades the measure of their personal worth. If I make all A's, I'm an excellent person; B's, a good person; C's, a fair person; D's, a poor person; F's, a failure in life.

Granted, school is important. Every student ought to try to get all the education he can and do his best to learn. But, in the final analysis, remember that academic knowledge is not the most important thing in life. My wife was caught up in this overemphasis on grades. She graduated from high school eighth out of a class of 500. But she admits now that if she had it to do over again, she would do it differently. Why? Because there is a high price that must be paid to make exceptional grades. We can get so caught up in studying that we don't have time for other things—like developing socially and spiritually.

Developing one's relationship with the Lord is far more important than getting all A's. The prophet

Jeremiah wrote over 2500 years ago, "Thus says the Lord, 'Let not a wise man boast of his wisdom, and let not the mighty man boast of his might, let not a rich man boast of his riches; but let him who boasts boast of this, that he understands and knows Me . . .'" (Jer. 9:23, 24). Far more important than gaining book knowledge is gaining spiritual knowledge of God. When you do this, you'll find that you gain a kind of wisdom that you could not learn at school (see Acts 4:13).

Material Possessions

The world says that material possessions make you important. According to advertisers, if you have fancy clothes, a motorcycle, a shiny new car, an expensive stereo, and have unlimited money to travel, then you're automatically accepted and liked.

These things may be nice, but in God's eternal value system they count for very little. God says, "Do not lay up for yourselves treasures upon earth, where moth and rust destroy, and where thieves break in and steal. But lay up for yourselves treasures in heaven, where neither moth nor rust destroys, and where thieves do not break in or steal; for where your treasure is, there will your heart be also" (Matt. 6:19–21).

We have just looked at five things that the world considers essential to being a "somebody." All these things are external, and they have nothing to do with inner character. Man looks at the outward appearance, but God looks at the heart. And we will go a long way toward developing a healthy self-image when we take our focus off these external things and begin to focus on developing inner character and a relationship with God.

God Made You the Way You Are

The third step in building a healthy self-image is to realize that God gives us our gifts, talents, and physical appearance. David writes:

> For Thou didst form my inward parts;
> Thou didst weave me in my mother's womb.
> I will give thanks to Thee,
> for I am fearfully and wonderfully made;
> Wonderful are Thy works,
> And my soul knows it very well.
> My frame was not hidden from Thee,
> When I was made in secret,
> And skillfully wrought in the depths of the earth.
> Thine eyes have seen my unformed substance;
> And in Thy book they were all written,
> The days that were ordained for me,
> When as yet there was not one of them
> (Ps. 139:13–16).

When we complain about our gifts or our appearance, we are in effect saying, "God, you made a mistake when you made me." But God didn't make a mistake. He had a *purpose* in making us the way we are.

This includes the things that we consider "defects." The apostle Paul had some sort of defect, which many scholars believe was an eye disease. Three times Paul prayed that God might take away this defect, this "thorn" (II Cor. 12:7–9). Three times God said no. But God did show Paul *why* He had given him the defect. It was given to keep Paul from exalting himself, to keep Paul from being proud. In the same way, God has a purpose in making us as we are. He even has a purpose in allowing those things that we consider "defects," for there are no accidents with God. It was God who formed us in our mother's womb (Ps. 139:13).

What then should we do about those physical things we don't like about ourselves? The answer is simple. We should simply accept what we can't change. God made me this way. I can't change it. Therefore I accept that God had a purpose in making me this way.

Abraham Lincoln learned this lesson early, and it was one of the reasons he went on to become one of the greatest men in history. Once, during the famous Lincoln/Douglas debates in Illinois, Senator Douglas accused Lincoln of being "two-faced." Lincoln pointed to his face and said, "It's the face my Maker gave me, and, for better or for worse, the only one I have. Now do you think I would go around holding it up in front of you if I had another one?" The audience broke out in applause, recognizing Lincoln's wit and self-accepting attitude.

Set a Goal To Excel at Something

The fourth step in building a healthy self-image is to find something that you enjoy doing and seek to excel in it. It greatly builds your confidence to know that you excel in something. Leon Spinks, the heavyweight boxer, tells the story that his father once punished him by suspending him from a nail and administering a beating. The father continually reminded young Spinks and anyone else who would listen that his son would "never amount to anything." Spinks recalls, "That became my thing ... to be somebody."[2] Spinks made up his mind that he was going to be somebody, and he accomplished that goal by excelling in boxing.

I firmly believe that you can do almost anything you want to do and can be anyone you want to be—*if* you are willing to pay the price. I heard about a man who came up to a concert pianist after hearing him play and said, "I'd give anything to play like you!" The pianist replied, "No you wouldn't. Would you give twelve hours a day to practice? Would you deny every other area of your life to excel on the piano?"

But if you are willing to pay the price, you *can* do anything. Strike the words, "I can't" from your vocabulary. When we say, "I can't," we really are saying, "I won't. I'm afraid I'll fail." Sure, you may fail. But when you keep on trying you can overcome the things you once failed at.

For years I tried to water-ski and failed. But I kept trying, and just recently, I succeeded! That really built my confidence. Also, I used to be deathly afraid to speak in front of people. I remember one time in high school I was supposed to read a paragraph to my high school English class. I was so frightened that my mouth was frozen. I just stood there shaking, unable to speak a word. But through the years I kept

2. *Time*, Feb. 27, 1978. p. 77

trying, and today I can speak with ease in front of many people—I even enjoy it!

Don't ever underestimate the power of God. With men, it may be impossible, but with God anything is possible. Dream big dreams, and then work hard to fulfill those dreams—all the while trusting God to help you. You *can* be a somebody. You *can* change. You *can* do what you didn't think was possible. Set goals, and as you accomplish those goals you'll discover your confidence growing. You'll begin to respect yourself, and your self-image will improve. Why not begin today?

Improve What You Can

There are some things that you can do to make yourself a more attractive person. As your self-image improves, you will become more attractive to the opposite sex.

Correct any correctable physical defects you may have. If you have crooked teeth, get braces. If you have a minor acne problem, concentrate on keeping your face clean. If you have a serious acne problem, see a dermatologist. If you are overweight, exercise and watch your diet. If you have a speech problem, see a speech therapist. All these physical problems and many more can be corrected with a little work.

Dress as fashionably as possible (your friends will tell you what looks good on you). Wear your hair attractively, and keep it neat and cut. These things will contribute to making you feel better about yourself and thus improve your self-image.

Do What You Know Is Right

James says, "Therefore, to one who knows the right thing to do, and does not do it, to him it is sin" (James 4:17). If we disobey God, we will feel guilty, and will begin to dislike ourselves—even hate ourselves. But as Meier writes, "Self-worth comes from doing what we know is right, and not doing those things that we believe are wrong."[3] If we see that our conduct is good, and according to God's will, our consciences will be clear, and we will also gain a healthy self-respect.

It is hoped that these six steps will help you to build a better self-image. Remember, before you can really be free to love others, you must first love yourself.

Discussion Questions

1. What don't you like about yourself? What do you like?
2. Study Psalm 139:13–16 very carefully. List three things that these verses tell us about how God made us.
3. Is there anyone in the Bible with a poor self-image? A good self-image?
4. What are two things you can do to improve your physical appearance?
5. Complete the following sentence: "I like myself because _____."
6. How should knowing that God made us the way we are and that He accepts us affect our self-image?

3. Paul Meier, *Christian Child-Rearing and Personality Development*, p. 39.

4

How to Know If You Are in Love

Some time ago, Hugh Hefner, the "Playboy King," was interviewed on the David Frost Show. David Frost asked one penetrating question that really struck me. He said, "Hugh, now that you've got everything that a man could possible want—all the fame, and success, and women—what would you like now?" There was a long pause as the camera zoomed in for a closeup of Hefner. Then Hefner slowly replied, "David, I'd give everything I own to find . . . true love." Here was a man who had everything that the world could offer, and yet he had not found true love.

People are searching desperately for love. Just recently I was asked to visit a widow who had tried to commit suicide. She had told her neighbor earlier that she was so lonely she just could not stand it. Teenager Samantha Clare of London was also searching for love—but gave up. Her suicide note ended with, "I wish someone would really love me!"

We all need love. As a matter of fact, we were *born* with an inner need for love. This was scientifically proven during World War II in an experiment by a German researcher named René Spitz. Spitz experimented with a number of infants in a European foundling home. The infants were allowed to stay with their mothers during the first three months of life and developed normally. Then they were separated from their mothers and cared for by nurses. They were fed well, got good medical attention, but received very little love and affection from the busy nurses. 30 percent of the babies died of malnutrition during the first year, and most of the survivors became permanently and severely retarded. You see, we cannot live without love.[1]

What Love Is Not

What, then, is this elusive thing called love that everyone so desperately needs? Hollywood and our TV soap operas lead us to believe that real love is is expressed by the following little story.

> I am a very attractive and lovable person, fascinating and desirable in every way. But I man-

1. Paul Meier, *Christian Child-Rearing and Personality Development,* pp. 114–15.

aged to go unnoticed for a long time. The reason for that was that the one and only person in this universe had not come my way. There was one made just for me and for no other, and at the right moment he was to come into my life. Then suddenly he appeared! In that moment our eyes met and I knew he was for me. He was my dream, my inspiration! He had everything! He was tall, tan, and terrific! We kissed and I knew that I could not live without him. This was love, because I was tingling with excitement all over. How could anything else be important but this? We would live only for each other in perfect bliss. If there had been any doubt, all doubt vanished when we held each other close. This is what I had longed for all my life. He made me feel so good. Love had brought me my ideal. There could be no reason to wait a moment longer. With his great sense of humor I knew we would never disagree about anything. Our love for each other would hurdle all obstacles as though they were nothing. Brought together by the hand of fate, we must obey and marry before it is too late! You dare not put off love for it might die if not acted on right now.

And so they married and lived happily ever after in the delightful ecstasy of marital bliss![2]

But this "Cinderella Syndrome," when the girl is waiting on her Prince Charming, is not real love. It is better called "infatuation," and there is a vast difference between it and real love.

2. Dwight H. Small, *Design for Christian Marriage* (Old Tappan, N. J.: Revell, 1971), p. 131.

First, infatuation is a feeling; real love involves a commitment also. Infatuation is just love of emotion. Real love, though, is love of devotion. Only the emotions are affected in infatuation, but in real love both the emotions and the will are involved.

Second, a person "falls into" infatuation, but "grows into" real love. Guys, have you ever seen a girl who was so beautiful that you thought you'd faint? As soon as you saw her you could hardly swallow, your heart started beating fast, and all you could think about was meeting that girl. Girls, have you ever gone to class and discovered that there was this new guy there who was the most handsome guy you've ever seen? You didn't hear a thing the teacher said that whole class period because all you could think of was that good-looking guy two rows over. This is infatuation! It is something that can strike instantly. It is based totally on physical attraction; often you have never even met the person you're infatuated with. It is very easy to become infatuated.

Please don't get me wrong. I'm not saying that infatuation is bad. As a matter of fact, it is very pleasurable. You can't prevent yourself from being infatuated at times, since infatuation is mostly biological. My point is that you need to be able to recognize it for what it is when it strikes. Don't call it love—call it infatuation. When you throw the word *love* around you make it cheap and common. Avoid telling someone that you love him or her unless you really mean it. A rock group of the sixties, The Doors, had a song that went, "Hello, I love you, won't you tell me your name?". That song reflects how cheap the word *love* has become today. The song is not about love; it is about physical attraction and infatuation.

I decided while I was dating that I wouldn't tell a girl that I loved her unless I was willing to marry her. I don't think that everyone should go that far, but I do think that you should only use the word *love* to mean something very special.

I am occasionally asked by high school students if I believe in love at first sight. I always answer, "No, I believe in infatuation at first sight but not love at first sight." Love is something that requires time and commitment. Genuine love can grow out of infatuation, but I don't think there is such a thing as love at first sight.

Third, infatuation is basically selfish where real love is basically selfless. In the final analysis, infatuation is more interested in satisfying itself and the "feeling" than it is in the other person. Infatuation is "in love with love" rather than in love with another person. There is a popular song with the lyrics, "I want you, I need you, but there ain't no way that I'm ever gonna love you—but don't be sad, 'cause two out of three ain't bad." Those lines reflect a totally selfish attitude—only interested in getting, not giving.

Real love, though, is primarily interested in the other person. It seeks to give instead of get. Love unselfishly seeks the highest good for the other person. Love is a four-letter word spelled g-i-v-e. God's love is like this. Do you remember John 3:16? "For God so loved the world that He *gave*...."

This does not mean that you are totally interested *only* in the other's welfare and think nothing of yourself. This is impossible. But it does mean that you are deeply concerned about this person, even to the point of sacrificing your interests in favor of his or hers.

Fourth, infatuation is weakened by time and separation where real love is strengthened by time and separation. When I was engaged, I was separated from my fiancée for ten weeks during the summer. I knew that this would be the crucial test of our relationship. Would my commitment to her grow stronger during our separation, or would I begin to desire to date other girls? Always in the past, when I was separated from a girlfriend for any length of time I found my heart wandering, and I started wanting to date other girls. However, that summer of being separated from my fiancée confirmed to me the rightness of our engagement. During the period of separation my love and commitment to her grew instead of weakened. Real love is like that.

This does not mean that there will be no pain in separation. On the contrary, there is great pain in separation if you are truly in love. That summer when I was separated from Rhonda, I had to fight depression and loneliness all the time. But even that pain confirmed to me the fact that I loved her and needed her.

The Characteristics of Love
I Corinthians 13:4-8

Have you ever tried to define love? It is difficult, isn't it? Every definition that we come up with seems to somehow fall short. But there is one definition that has stood the test of time. It was written almost two thousand years ago by the apostle Paul and is found in I Corinthians 13. There Paul gives the clearest and most complete definition of love ever penned. As a prism breaks light into its many colorful parts, so in I Corinthians 13 Paul breaks love into its many wonderful and magnificent parts. Let us look at some of the characteristics of love that Paul lists.

Love Is Patient

The word translated "patient" means to wait patiently for the fulfillment of expectations. The same word is used in Hebrews 6:15 to describe Abraham waiting patiently on God to fulfill His promise. It is used also in James 5:7, 8 to exhort oppressed believers to wait patiently for the return of Christ.

I Corinthians 13 teaches that real love exhibits patience. It is very easy to become impatient with one another about little things. I have a problem in this area. I tend to be a perfectionist, and if everything doesn't go exactly right, I often become impatient. I remember one time I was talking to Rhonda, my wife, before we were married. She had had a bad week and was complaining to me. I thought she was being very negative and hard-to-get-along-with. Usually I react to this by becoming angry and impatient with her for being so grouchy. This time, though, I was very patient and understanding. Later that evening I took the opportunity to point out to her how patient I'd been with her earlier. She said, "Yes, but why aren't you that way all the time?" She was right—real love is patient.

Love is patient in another way also. Have you ever met someone you liked so much that you wanted to push the relationship and make it progress faster? Sure you have! Love, however, is willing to give a relationship time to grow at a natural pace. It does not push the relationship but is willing to wait for the relationship to grow at a rate that is satisfactory to both parties. Jacob is a great example of this. He was willing to wait patiently for seven years to marry Rachael. How many of us would be willing to wait seven years for someone?

Love Is Kind

Love seeks to encourage and build up others. It respects the feelings and emotions of others. It finds its greatest satisfaction in making others happy. It is tragic to see so many relationships in which people are downright unkind to one another. Couples are continuously hurting one another, intentionally and unintentionally. But love seeks to make the other person feel good. The whole Song of Solomon is an example of this. All through Song of Solomon, Solomon goes out of his way to treat his lover kindly and to encourage her.

Kindness is not something that comes naturally. It must be cultivated. Here are a few practical suggestions on how to treat your girlfriend or boy friend kindly.

1.   Give one another things. Guys, you will never understand *how much* girls appreciate little gifts. Girls aren't so impressed with how much money you

spend on them as they are by the fact that you were thinking of them. It makes a girl glow inside when she knows that you've been secretly planning her happiness.

May I say a word here about flowers. Guys, you probably won't understand this, but take it by faith—girls flip over flowers! To a girl, flowers are the greatest thing in the world, because they are an expression of your love.

Girls, don't you neglect to give him things and do little things for him also. I remember when I was in college that a Christian sister tore out a page from a Charlie Brown coloring book, colored it for me, and anonymously sent it to me. It was a picture of Lucy looking up at Charlie Brown and the caption read, "Little sisters need Big Brothers." That little picture made my week! Girls, if you love a guy, go out of your way to make him feel special. Do little things for him like washing his car when he's not around or baking him some cookies.

2.   Compliment one another. Guys, be sure to magnify your girl's strengths and to minimize her weaknesses. In the Song of Solomon we find both Solomon and his lover constantly complimenting one another. A girl needs to be told that she is pretty or that a certain dress really looks good on her. If your girl friend spends four hours getting prettied up for you on a date and you don't even mention how she looks, then *look out!* If your girl cooks well or plays tennis well or does anything else well, you need to be thoughtful enough to compliment her.

Girls, you need to compliment your boyfriend also. Let me tell you a little secret about guys. Guys have *big egos*. My advice to you is not to fight it, but if he looks good or does something well, tell him so.

3. Listen to one another. Pay close attention to what each of you has to say and make each other feel that what each says is important. (God gave you *two* ears and *one* mouth for a reason!)

4. Treat one another special in public. Compliment and encourage one another in the presence of others.

5. Guys, take your girl friend out occasionally. I realize that if you are dating steadily it is impossible to spend money on her all the time unless your father is president of an oil company, but girls get tired of watching TV with you every weekend. I fell into this rut when I was in college with a girl that I was dating. Every Friday night our big date was to snuggle up on her couch and watch "The Friday Night Frights," a weekly horror movie hosted by a man sitting in a coffin named Dead Earnest. Just recently that girl met my wife and asked if I was still cheap! The point is, guys, try to be creative in your dating. There are lots of things you can do that don't cost a lot of money.

Love Is Not Jealous

The word *jealous* is also used in Acts 5:17 and 13:44, 45 to describe the anger a person feels when his place of popularity or respect is being lost to another. Proverbs 27:4 says, "Wrath is fierce and anger is a flood, but who can stand before jealousy?"

Jealousy usually indicates an insecure and immature heart. Love wants the best for the other, but jealousy is possessive. Jealousy is reflected in the childish statement, "Well, if he is going to talk to her, then he can just forget about me!"

Often, one person wants to totally possess the other and to restrict his or her relationships with others. A jealous person gets uptight whenever his or her date even talks to someone of the opposite sex. Needless to say, this is not love.

We all are tempted to jealousy at times. I've found that the best solution is to *pray* for the person you are jealous of. It is hard to remain angry at someone when you are praying for them.

Love Does Not Brag

Love is not a windbag and is not anxious to impress. Often a guy will brag to a girl, trying to impress her so that she will like him. A truly great person, however, does not need to exalt himself. Others will exalt him.

Love Is Not Arrogant

Love is not conceited, boastful, cocky, or stuck-up. Love, instead, is humble and has a servant attitude.

Sometimes a guy may come across to a girl with an "I can take you or leave you" attitude (girls can come across this way too!). His demeanor implies, "You ought to be thankful that somebody as neat as me is dating you." Of course, this is not love.

Love Does Not Act Unbecomingly

This means that love does not behave disgracefully, dishonorably, or indecently. It does not embarrass others by its actions. It is characterized by tact and sensitivity.

I think this also means that love should have good manners. This may not be too popular today, but I believe that all girls appreciate courtesy and gentlemanliness. Be sure to do little things like opening doors for your girl, or offering her your arm when you walk together. My grandmother tells the story of a fellow who dated her many years ago. He failed to open the car door for her, so she sat there until he did. That young man learned a hard lesson in manners that evening.

Love Does Not Seek Its Own

This is the heart of love. Love is other-centered rather than self-centered. Love says, "I love you, I want to give to you." Selfishness says, "I love me, I want you!"

Love Is Not Provoked

This means that love has a long fuse. It does not become irritated and angry. It is not easily offended. Unfortunately, a short temper is often a vice of even the most virtuous—Moses, for example. But even Moses had to pay a terrible price for not controlling his temper. Proverbs 29:11 says, "A fool always loses his temper, but a wise man holds it back." Incidentally, Proverbs 22:24 advises us not to "go out" with someone who can't control his temper.

Love Will Not Take into Account a Wrong Suffered

This is a *must* for a successful relationship. If a guy is not willing to forgive and forget when his girlfriend is ten minutes late, he is not exhibiting love. Love doesn't hold grudges when it has been wronged. It doesn't remain resentful. Henry Ward Beecher once wrote, "Keep a fair-sized cemetery in your backyard in which to bury the faults of your friends." Love is not "keeping a list, checking it twice, gonna find out who's been naughty and nice." Love *forgets* past failures and sins.

Love Does Not Rejoice in Unrighteousness, but Rejoices in the Truth

This phrase is difficult to interpret, but I think Paul means that love cannot sympathize with what is evil. Love is not silent but speaks when the other is in the wrong. One application of this is that a girl should not tolerate a boy who constantly breaks traffic laws or cheats in school.

Love Always Covers

This word *cover* means to pass over in silence, to keep confidential. Love is patient with the faults of others. It doesn't criticize and broadcast to the world the faults of others. Love is there even when it knows the other is not perfect. God's love is like this, for God loves us even though He knows that we are still sinful and imperfect.

Love Always Believes

This means that love believes the best of the other person. George Sweeting, president of Moody Bible Institute, writes, "Love takes the kindest view possible of people and circumstances. Love searches for what is good and gives the benefit of the doubt."[3] I once heard Jack Taylor, a popular conference speaker, say, "Don't love her for what she appears to be, but for what she will be when He appears."

Love Always Hopes

Love is always optimistic. Love trusts God that the relationship will be even better in the future.

Love Always Perseveres

Love always stands its ground and holds out. It will outlast anything. It will even love in the face of unreturned love. Perhaps the greatest example of this in the Bible is Hosea and Gomer. Gomer became a prostitute—and yet Hosea still loved her! Real love will persevere through all sorts of trials and stresses.

Love Never Fails

Love cannot be shaken. It never ceases. It is always there. Nothing can cause you to cease loving if it is real love.

3. George Sweeting, *Love Is the Greatest*.

Conclusion

There is a vast difference between love and infatuation. Television, movies, radio, and a host of other sources all seek to tell us that love is a romantic, gushy feeling. But in I Corinthians 13, God tells us what real love is. Love is a genuine commitment of one's heart, mind, and soul to another person. This commitment seeks the best for the other person and seeks to give to that other person. Obviously, this kind of love does not come naturally to us, for we are basically selfish people. Real love must be worked at and must be cultivated, but the rewards are well worth the effort. As we conclude this discussion on love, let me challenge you as Paul challenged the Corinthians to "pursue love" in your relationships with others (I Cor. 14:1).

Discussion Questions

1. Study Judges 14:1–3. Is this genuine love or infatuation? Why?
2. Study Genesis 29:18–21. Is this genuine love or infatuation? Why?
3. Study I Corinthians 13:4–8. Pick out one attribute of love that really speaks to you and explain *why* it speaks to you.
4. Study I John 4:7–12. List three things that this passage teaches you about love.

5

What About
Dating Non-Christians?

The issue of dating non-Christians is probably the most controversial issue that we will discuss in this book on Christian dating. Before we start on this very touchy issue, let me encourage you to keep an open mind throughout the discussion. Please do not reject what I say until you think it through.

Before we start, let me once again encourage you to honestly examine your attitudes. Like Paul, is your sole ambition in life to be *pleasing to the Lord*? Do you really want God's will and God's *very best* in your dating life?

In John 14:15, Jesus said, "If you love Me, you will keep My commandments." God has given some clear guidelines in the Bible. You must ask yourself, "Do I really love God and want to please Him strongly enough to obey these guidelines—even though they may be hard?"

We need to understand why God gives commands in Scripture so that we don't react to biblical guidelines out of ignorance. Personally, I can't stand for someone to tell me what to do. Are you like that? Human nature is like that. If we are told outright not to do something, we tend to react and to go ahead and do it just to prove our independence. If I were to put a sign on a storefront window downtown that said, "Please don't throw a brick through this window," what would happen? Someone would throw a brick through the window, of course! We need to beware of reacting to God's commands in such a foolish manner.

We can be assured that if God tells us not to do something, then He has a very good reason. God is not a divine killjoy who searches the earth for those having a good time, shouting down, "Hey you, cut that out!" No, when God gives us commandments, it is for a very good reason. First, He gives us commandments to *protect* us from hurting ourselves. He is all-knowing, and can see that certain things will cause us great problems on down the road. Second, God gives us commands to *provide* the very best for us. His commandments are an expression of His love, to insure that we get the very best.

Dating Non-Christians:
Biblical Principles

Sue Ellen was a vivacious senior in high school who had just recently discovered the Lord. I was a non-

Christian at the time but was attracted to her and to the quality of life that she exhibited. I never had the opportunity to date her, because she was going steady with another guy, but she did invite me to some Christian youth meetings sponsored by Campus Crusade for Christ. Eventually, she shared the gospel with me and I trusted Jesus Christ to save me and to forgive my sins. I began to grow in the Lord, but Sue Ellen began to slip in her relationship with God. She broke up with the Christian guy that she had been dating for three years and began to date a young, non-Christian lawyer. She had just graduated from high school and this guy was a sharp lawyer, and he simply snowed her. She fell in love (or at least became infatuated) and married him three months later. Meanwhile, however, she was growing colder and colder toward spiritual things. Their marriage was rocky, and less than a year later they were divorced. By this time Sue Ellen was hardened by the world and utterly cold toward the Lord.

Several months later, a friend and I went over to her apartment to talk to her about her relationship with Christ. She actually asked us to leave her apartment and stop talking to her about Jesus. She didn't want to hear anything about it. It is now some six years later and, as far as I know, she is still apathetic and cold toward spiritual things. Sue Ellen's experience is only one of many, many examples I have seen when dating a non-Christian ruined the spiritual life of a person. I've worked with high school students for seven years and have seen that dating a non-Christian is one of the major reasons for losing interest in spiritual things.

There are no Bible passages that say, "Thou shalt not date a non-Christian." But there are many passages that teach that a Christian should not *marry* a non-believer. Let's look at II Corinthians 6:14 for example. It reads, "Do not be bound together with unbelievers; for what partnership have righteousness and lawlessness, or what fellowship has light with darkness?" The phrase, "Do not be bound together" is translated, "Be ye not unequally yoked" in the King James Version. If you hitched an ox and a horse together to pull a wagon, several things would probably happen. The animals would probably go around in circles, for the horse's legs are longer. They would also probably fight and bite at each other, and pull in different directions trying to get away from one another. Whatever the case, you wouldn't get much work done.

This is the way it often is when a Christian is married to a non-Christian. They either go in circles in their relationship, fight with one another, or pull in different directions. Paul's picture is vivid and the point is obvious. It is not wise to marry a non-believer.

Paul also warns against marrying a non-believer in several other verses. In I Corinthians 7:39, Paul points out that a widow is free to remarry, but *only in the Lord* (i.e., only a believer.) In I Corinthians 9:5, Paul says that he has the right to take a *believing* wife (literally a "sister" as his wife.) This implies that it is wrong to take an unbelieving wife.

Human beings are composed of body, soul, and spirit. When a Christian marries a non-Christian, the most that they can have is two-thirds of a relationship:

Christian	Non-Christian
Body ⟷	Body
Soul ⟷	Soul
Spirit ⟷✕⟷	Spirit

A Christian and a non-Christian can relate physically (body). They can relate emotionally and intellectually (soul). But it is impossible for them to relate spiritually because a non-Christian is spiritually dead. This is especially significant when you stop to consider that the spirit is the most important part of a person. The spiritual relationship is intended by God to regulate the physical and emotional areas. If you are not right spiritually it will hurt you in every other area.

A husband and wife need a complete, whole relationship. Marriage has tremendous pressures, and marriage partners need all their resources going for them when they get married. Recent statistics show that 40 percent of all marriages end in divorce. And yet I recently heard Billy Graham say that only one in 400 Christian marriages ends in divorce, when there is prayer and family devotions in the home. What makes the difference? Obviously, it is the spiritual area. Can you see now how foolish it is to marry a non-Christian?

But young people often object, "Sure, I believe that I should *marry* a Christian, but why can't I date a non-Christian? Just because I date someone does not mean that I am going to marry him (or her). If I date only Christians then I won't get to date at all because there are no Christian guys (or girls) around." My reply to this objection is that you begin habits and patterns in dating that carry over to marriage. If you usually date non-Christians, then chances are you will marry a non-Christian. Once we get seriously and emotionally involved in a relationship, we have difficulty controlling our hearts and we lose spiritual discernment. There is a very predictable process of spiritual decline that I have seen occur time after time when a Christian begins to date a non-Christian. I think it might be helpful if I shared it with you.

Satan Tempts

Satan will bring a really attractive person into your life. Listen, *Satan's temptations are tempting.* He will not bring some ugly person along who doesn't interest you anyway. No, Satan will bring someone along toward whom you are really attracted. Girls, perhaps it will be that football player who is so popular. Guys, may be it will be some cute cheerleader who starts flirting with you. Whatever the case, this person will seem perfect in every way except that he or she is cold toward spiritual things.

You Rationalize

Instead of resisting the temptation (I Peter 5:8), you begin to rationalize your feelings about this person. "Just this once . . . ." "Well, it's better than sitting at home." "He *is* a nice guy." "Maybe I can witness to him."

You Give In and Go Out

You start spending time with this person. You may even greatly enjoy the relationship, but it is not on a

spiritual plane. Often you find yourself getting involved in a deep physical relationship very quickly.

You Fall in Love (or Become Infatuated)

It is amazing how often this happens. I had one good
friend who was a strong Christian and was one of the
Christian leaders on her campus. She told me later
that she had never really fallen for a guy in her life
(and she was extremely beautiful.) Some of us guys
thought that she had a heart of stone! The summer of
her junior year she went home to her small hometown
to work for the summer. There was no real Christian
fellowship for her to become involved in and so it was
a dry summer. One weekend a guy at work asked her
out. She didn't have anything else to do so she went
out with him, even though he was not a Christian. You
guessed it—she fell in love with him!

You Must Choose Between that Person and God

You must make a choice, either consciously or un-
consciously, between God and that person. If you
choose God, you will be hurt emotionally because
you must break off the relationship. But if you choose
the other person, then you will be hurt spiritually
because you are putting another person before God.

Rapid Spiritual Decline

If you choose another person before God, then it will
lead to a rapid spiritual decline. Your heart will
become hard and cold toward spiritual things.

We see this process of spiritual decline clearly illus-
trated by Solomon in I Kings 11. Solomon disobeyed

God and married foreign wives who did not believe in the Lord God Jehovah. The result was that "his wives turned his heart away after other gods; and his heart was not wholly devoted to the Lord his God, as the heart of David his father had been" (I Kings 11:4). This is why it is so important to "guard your affections" (Prov. 4:23, Living Bible). Once we make a commitment in our hearts to love someone, then we've got problems.

Please don't misunderstand me. I am not saying that we should not have anything to do with non-Christians. Not at all. We have a sober responsibility to win the lost to Christ (Col. 4:5, 6), which is difficult to do if we are not even friends with them. As a matter of fact, Paul tells us in I Corinthians 5:9, 10 that it is impossible not to associate with non-believers as long as we live on earth. But, our *close* friendships and dating relationships should be with believers. Not only is there the danger that non-believers will turn our hearts away from the Lord, but there is also the danger that they will corrupt our morals. Paul tells us in I Corinthians 15:33 that bad company corrupts good morals. The reason for this is that we tend to take on the characteristics of those whose company we enjoy and whose attitudes we respect. We find an example of this in Proverbs 22:24, 25 where we are warned, "Do not associate with a man given to anger; or go with a hot-tempered man, lest you learn his ways, and find a snare for yourself."

Discussion Questions

1. Read I Kings 3. What was Solomon's spiritual condition when he first became king? (see especially v. 3).

2. What is Solomon's warning to the people in I Kings 8:61 and why is it significant?

3. Read Deuteronomy 17:14–17 (especially vv. 16, 17), and then read I Kings 10:24—11:8. In what three ways did Solomon disobey God?

4. What do you think happened between I Kings 8 and I Kings 11 which caused Solomon to disobey God? (speculate!)

5. In I Kings 11:3, 4 we read that Solomon's foreign wives turned his heart away from the Lord. What do you think this means?

6. Does I Kings 11:3, 4 apply to dating relationships between Christians and non-Christians? If so, how?

7. How did God judge Solomon's sin? (I Kings 11:9–13).

6

What Makes a Great Dating Relationship?

In the last chapter we saw that it was displeasing to God for us to date non-Christians. I hope you have now decided before the Lord to date only believers. However, even if you vow to date only believers, that does not mean that all your relationships will necessarily be pleasing to God. There are many things that go into making a dating relationship God-honoring. In this chapter we want to ask four questions that zero in on the most important requirements. These things are not optional, but are central to pleasing the Lord in your dating relationships. As a child of God who really desires to please your Father, I'm sure that you will consider these things carefully. The purpose is not to limit your fun in dating, but instead to give you the greatest possible fulfillment in your dating life.

Are You Both Controlled by the Holy Spirit?

Not only is it important to avoid close relationships with non-Christians, but it is also important to avoid close relationships with those who profess to be Christians and yet are not fully committed to the Lord and filled with the Spirit. The reason for this is that our close friends will seriously affect our spiritual condition. If our friends have a heart for God, it is much easier for us to have a heart for God. By the same token, it is very easy for a close friend's cold heart to be contagious and to cause us to become more interested in worldly things.

We see this principle stressed constantly in the Bible. David said in Psalm 119:63, "I am a companion of all those who fear Thee." In II Timothy 2:22 Paul exhorts Timothy to "flee from youthful lusts, and pursue righteousness, faith, love and peace, *with those who call on the Lord from a pure heart*." Are our closest friends those who call on the Lord from a pure heart? Only when we have companions like that are we really able to flee youthful lusts and to pursue after righteousness, faith, love, and peace.

In I Corinthians 5:11–13, Paul gives a strong command concerning our relationships with professing Christians whose deeds are not spiritual. Paul says that we should not even *associate* with someone who claims to be a brother and yet lives an evil, sinful life. These are strong but necessary words, because such a person is dishonoring the name of Christ by his inconsistent life. Once again, the reason that we should avoid people like this is that "bad company corrupts good morals" (I Cor. 15:33).

In II Thessalonians 3:6, Paul gives a similar exhortation. He commands in the name of the Lord Jesus Christ that we "keep aloof from every brother who leads an unruly life and not according to the tradition which you received from us."

We must realize, however, that just because someone is Spirit-filled does not mean that he will be perfect. Beware of searching for the perfect person—you will most certainly be disappointed!

Do Your Parents Approve of the Relationship?

The importance of parental approval is not a very popular thing to teach to young people, but I believe it is Scriptural. A young person's parents have the last word in his or her life. As a young person, you are under the absolute authority of your parents. This teaching is found in many places in the Bible. In Ephesians 6:1, children are commanded to "obey your parents in the Lord." And one of the great commandments God gave to the children of Israel was, "Honor your father and your mother" (Exod. 20:12). In Colossians 3:20, Paul again exhorts children to "be obedient to your parents in all things, for this is well-pleasing to the Lord." In Luke 2:51, we see the example of Jesus, for Luke says that Jesus "continued in subjection" to His mother and father. If Jesus who was God obeyed His earthly parents, how much more should we who are mere humans obey our parents!

One of the major themes of the Book of Proverbs is obedience of children to their parents. In Proverbs

6:20–24 we see that obedience to the teaching of our parents will keep us from getting involved in immoral relationships. In Proverbs 30:17 we see the solemn warning that "the eye that mocks a father, and scorns a mother, the ravens of the valley will pick it out, and the young eagles will eat it." This is not to be taken literally, of course, but it does teach the solemn principle that the rebellious son or daughter will pay dearly for his or her disobedience.

We should obey our parents, even apart from the fact that God commands it, because our parents have far more maturity than we do and God desires to steer our actions through them. Proverbs 13:1 says that a wise son will accept his father's guidance, but a foolish son will reject it.

How Should My Parents Affect My Dating Life?

The implications for dating are obvious. Our parents should have the final word concerning who we date, where we go, what we do, and when we are to be home at night. This isn't popular and it may sound tyrannical, but it is the obvious conclusion from the Bible verses we have looked at. If your parents don't approve of the person you're dating, then you need to accept the fact that God is telling you not to date that person. If your parents tell you to be in at ten o'clock, then you should accept that God wants you to be in at ten o'clock. If your parents tell you they don't want you to go to a certain place on a date, then you need to accept that God is telling you that He doesn't want you to go there. Paul says in Ephesians

6:1 to obey your parents *in the Lord*. This means that you are to obey your parents *as to the Lord*. When your parents express their will to you, you are to accept it as the Lord's will for your life.

What If My Parents Are Not Christians?

Sometimes the objection is raised that a young person shouldn't have to obey his or her parents if they are not Christians. This is not true, however, because God can work through parents whether or not they are Christians.

What If They Are Unreasonable?

Some time ago a high school student came to me with a problem. She was dating a guy whom she liked a great deal. The problem was that her dad had forbidden her to hold hands or in any way express affection physically until she got married. The boy she was dating wanted to at least hold hands, and so did she. She faced a dilemma—she wanted to obey her father and she wanted to hold hands with this guy. She asked me what she should do. I agreed that her father was making some unreasonable demands on her, but I advised her to obey her father. I encouraged her to pray and ask God to change her father's mind if that was His will. I told her that if she wanted to talk to her father about why she thought he was unreasonable, that was all right, but she should be certain to assure him that she would still obey him even though she disagreed with him.

A principle that we need to understand here is that the best way to gain freedom is by obedience. Obedience to your parents builds their trust in you. In turn, this trust makes them willing to give you even more freedom.

What If My Parents Don't Care What I Do?

Some parents refuse to exercise authority over their children. They disobey their God-given responsibility as parents. If you have parents like this, you need then to seek to obey their *wishes* rather than their commands. Usually a parent will at least express how he feels about something. You need to listen for this. If you don't know how your parents feel, then ask, "Mom, what do you really think about Tom?"

When Do I Cease Being Under the Authority of My Parents?

Needless to say, there has to be a time when you are no longer under the absolute authority of your parents. Probably the best rule to follow is that you are under your parent's authority as long as you are living at home and/or are being financially supported by them. But even though there will come a time when you no longer must obey them, there will never come a time when you no longer must honor them. Even after you leave home and are totally independent of your parents, you still should seek their advice and try to please them as far as possible.

Does the Relationship Build You Up and Help Your Relationship with God?

God desires us to focus all our attention and energy toward loving and serving Him. Therefore, He wants our dating life to help us focus more on Him, rather than to turn our attention somewhere else. God's design is that a dating relationship should build us spiritually. The ideal is that as we get to know the person we are dating, we get to know God better, also.

Generally, a dating relationship will either help or hinder you spiritually. In order to help you work toward a spiritually encouraging relationship, I have included a few suggestions.

1. Ask yourself the following question: What is God desiring to do in his (or her) life and how can He use me to help? For example, several years ago I was dating a girl who was very shy about sharing her faith. One day, we were at a laundromat and I was talking about Christ with a lady. I turned to Pam and said, "Pam, why don't you share your experience with Jesus Christ with this woman?" Pam was scared, but she still gave a wonderful testimony. Later she thanked me for helping her to overcome her initial fear of sharing Christ.

2. See your date first as your brother or sister in Christ and only second as your date. In I Timothy 5:1, 2, Paul exhorts Timothy to look on younger men as brothers and on younger women as sisters. When we look at one another this way, it

will influence our behavior when we are together.

3. Be sure that you are pursuing your relationship
    with God first, and next your relationship with
    your boyfriend or girlfriend. Honestly ask your-
    self, Who is *really* most important to me? This is a
    very subtle temptation, and yet it can wreck a
    relationship spiritually.

4. Pray for one another. Be prayer partners. It is
    easy to pray for someone you care about, be-
    cause he or she is constantly in your thoughts.

5. Spend time together in prayer and Bible study.
    Guys, you need to initiate here—it is your re-
    sponsibility!

6. Encourage one another in your relationships
    with your parents. Do not encourage rebellion,
    but instead encourage one another to obedi-
    ence and to good attitudes.

Is the Relationship Morally Pure?

A morally impure relationship is sin and is clearly out
of the will of God. Many Scripture passages solemnly
warn young people against the sin of moral impurity.
We shall say much more about this later, but for the
time being, let it suffice to say that you are out of the
will of God if you are engaged in a deep premarital
physical relationship (I'll define what I mean by this
more clearly later.) If you find yourself involved in
such a relationship, God's Word to you is to either
clean it up or break off the relationship.

But I Won't Have Any Dates!

After looking at all the guidelines that we have shared in the last two chapters, perhaps you are thinking, "If I date by these standards, I'll never have a date." Perhaps, but is it not better not to date at all than to date out of the will of God?

Fortunately, though, I don't think that this will mean that you'll never be able to date. But there is an important spiritual principle that comes into play here. The principle is that if we seek God's best, then He'll bring His best. In Matthew 6:33, Jesus says, "But seek first His kingdom and His righteousness; and all these things shall be added to you." Again, in Psalm 84:11, we read, "No good thing does He withhold from those who walk uprightly." These verses clearly teach that if we seek God first and seek to obey Him, then He will provide everything that we need.

The Old Testament story of Ruth is a tremendous example of this. Ruth forsook her friends, her pagan gods, her nation, and what must have seemed to be all hopes of marriage to go to Israel with her mother-in-law Naomi and to accept the God of Israel. Yet God blessed Ruth and gave her a wonderful husband and a son. As a matter of fact, Jesus Christ was a descendant of Ruth and Boaz.

And so we see that God never forsakes those who seek Him first. Sure, you may have to sit home some Saturday nights. But be assured that God will bless your commitment not to lower your standards.

Will You Commit Yourself?

Are you willing to commit yourself before God to the five standards we have considered in the last two chapters?

1. I will not date a non-Christian.

2. I will only date someone who is Spirit-filled and will seek to allow the Holy Spirit to control my life also.

3. I will seek my parents' approval of those I date.

4. I will not settle for any relationship that does not build us both up spiritually.

5. I will strive to keep all my relationships morally pure.

Are you willing to yield your right to date to the Lord? Will you commit yourself to date only in His will? Right now, before we go any further, why don't you bow your head and commit this to the Lord?

Discussion Questions

1. Read Titus 2:2–8. What are the four age groups of people that this passage addresses?

2. According to Titus 2, what are the seven things that should characterize young married women?

3. What five things should characterize a godly young man? Define each of these in your own words.

4. Study Proverbs 31:10–31. List at least ten characteristics of an excellent wife from the passage.

5. If you could describe the woman in Proverbs 31 with one word, what would you call her? Why?

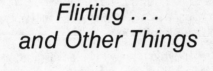

7

Flirting . . .
and Other Things

In this chapter we will deal with five practical problem areas associated with dating. Though the Bible doesn't have a lot to say about the areas that we will cover here, I have included them because they are so important. What we say in this lesson should be seen more as "useful advice" than "biblical commands."

How To Ask a Girl for a Date
(For Guys)

Often, the occasion of calling a new girl on the phone and asking her out was a time of great fear and trembling and gnashing of teeth for me. I can remember that I would rather have faced a ferocious alligator in hand-to-hand combat than call a girl for the first time. I have found that most guys have this same fear. I'd like to give you a little practical advice that might make it easier for you.

Sometimes it is easier to ask a girl out over the phone than it is to ask her out in person. You can conceal your nervousness over the phone much more easily than you can in person.

Begin the conversation with small talk rather than by immediately asking her out. This breaks the ice and also lets you "talk out" your nervousness. Usually the longer you talk to her, the more comfortable you will feel.

Be sure to tell her what you want her to do with you. Don't just call and say, "Hey, Judy, why don't we get together and bum around together Friday night?". Instead, specify what you want to do. "Judy, there is going to be a Christian concert Friday night and I thought you might like to go with me."

Be positive. Don't say, "You wouldn't want to go out with me Friday night, would you?" Be confident when you ask her out. If a girl senses that you don't expect her to accept the date, it makes her feel insecure and she may turn you down.

Avoid using the word "date." This is too formal and may make a girl uncomfortable. Perhaps the best way is to say something like this: "Jane, this is Joe. I'd really like to get together so that we can get to know each other better. Would you like to go to the church picnic with me next Saturday?"

How To (Discreetly) Attract a Guy's Attention (For Girls)

Some time ago my wife came to me with a problem. One of her best friends was very interested in a certain guy and really wanted him to ask her out. The guy and the girl were friends, but he had never asked her out and didn't date much. Anyway, this raised a problem—how does a girl let a guy know that she's interested in him without scaring him off?

Before we answer this, there is something very important that girls need to be aware of. When a guy asks a girl out, he always sticks his neck out and risks rejection. Since it is very discouraging to be turned down, a guy often will not take the initiative to ask a girl out unless he has a good reason to believe that she will accept. For this reason it is sometimes helpful for a girl to "encourage" a guy. There are several ways that you can do this.

You can communicate a great deal by your eyes. When you are at a meeting where he is, arrange to sit across from him. Look at him and try to catch his eye every now and then. He'll get the message! I heard of one guy who had his best friend sit next to him and whisper to him when a certain girl was looking at him! Of course, don't overdo it!

Pay close attention to him when he speaks. This shows him that you are really interested in what he has to say. A guy will notice this.

Get a friend to help you. Often a friend can pass on the information to the guy that you are interested in him. However, your friend must be tactful or you may be worse off than when you started.

Sometimes a double date arranged by a good friend can help. He may get a date for himself and then encourage the person you are interested in to ask you out. This is an especially good plan because double dates are often the best kind of first dates. You don't know one another very well and so a double date can really help conversation— especially if you are doubling with a fun, outgoing guy and girl.

Be around him as much as possible, without overdoing it. Make a point of being wherever he is. Voluntarily sit down next to him or sit across from him where you can catch his eye. A warning though—don't be too obvious! Don't let him get the idea that you are "chasing" him.

Ask him to help you with your homework. A guy is flattered whenever a girl asks him to help her.

Don't be too "easy to get." A basic principle of human nature is that we long for what we don't have and take for granted what we already have. For example, we have all known what it is to want something—say a car. But once the car is ours, it's no big deal any more. We almost immediately start wanting something else—a stereo, or a bigger car.

This principle applies in dating. If you seem a little out of reach, you are more desirable to the opposite sex. So if you like someone, don't throw yourself at him. Instead, play it cool. At all times keep your dignity and self-respect.

Pray and commit it to the Lord. This is most important. God is able to arrange circumstances and to
move men's hearts. Rely on God to arrange things if
this relationship is His will. But if nothing develops,
quietly accept it as His will.

How To Turn Down Dates

This can be a difficult problem for the Christian girl
who wants God's best. Non-Christians and carnal
Christian guys sometimes do call her up and ask her
out. She has settled in her heart that she doesn't want
to go out with these guys, but how does she turn
them down? What does she say? Also, how should
she turn down spiritual Christian guys that she simply is not attracted to? What is the best way to turn
down dates?

How To Turn Down Non-Christians and Carnal Christians

Let's look first at the problem of turning down dates
from non-Christians and carnal Christians. Obviously, there is a right way and a wrong way to turn
down dates. We will all agree that a girl shouldn't turn
down a guy by saying, "I'm sorry, I'm a Christian and
I can't go out with you." This sort of self-righteous
attitude may possibly turn him away from the Lord
forever.

When you turn down a non-Christian, you need to
communicate two things. First, communicate a loving and a humble spirit. The guy must not feel that
you are rejecting him as a person or that you feel that

you are better than he is. Second, I think it is important that you communicate *why* you won't go out with him. If he is a guy that you wouldn't want to go out with anyway, then don't bring in Christianity. Simply tell him that you're not interested in becoming involved in a dating relationship with him. But if his relationship with the Lord is the main thing that is keeping you from going out with him, then I think you ought to explain that. If you have Christian parents and have talked with them about this issue of dating non-Christians, then you might say, "I have made an agreement with my parents that I would date only guys that are committed to Jesus Christ. I don't know you well enough to know if you are or not. Why don't we get together and talk about it sometime?" This gives you a perfect opportunity to share your faith.

How To Turn Down Christians

How does a Christian girl turn down a date from a spiritual Christian guy? First, try to be gentle, but don't overly worry about hurting him. We Christian guys can take it. Oftentimes we really learn from being hurt and it causes us to have to lean upon the Lord for our strength and encouragement.

When you turn down a guy, don't say, "I really don't feel God is leading me to date you" unless you have truly sought God's will in the matter by serious prayer. So often we just use God as an excuse. After all, who can argue with God?

Perhaps the best thing to do is to be honest. Assure the guy that you really appreciate his friendship but that you don't feel good about getting involved in a dating relationship with him. Honesty is *always* the best policy. Never just put a guy off with excuses. Besides, it won't solve the problem anyway, because if the guy is really serious about dating you he'll just call back again and you'll have to keep putting him off. A friend of mine told me of a guy who kept calling her. She said that she kept putting him off with excuses until finally one afternoon he called and asked her to go out with him that evening. She told him that she couldn't go out with him because she had to wash her hair that evening. Well, he had heard that excuse before and so asked why she couldn't wash her hair another night. She replied, "I could, but since you called, I decided that tonight was the best night to wash it!" I think he got the message!

Take a Risk on a Date Sometimes

Girls, let me encourage you to sometimes take a risk with some spiritual guys that call you who may not seem to be the most desirable dates. Maybe the guy is shy and quiet or average-looking. But it could be that you might be God's instrument for helping some guy blossom. Sometimes the best "finds" are not outwardly obvious. Take a chance to get to know some Christian guy who is really interested in you. After all, aren't you glad that God took a chance on you!

The reason that I have to say this is that, sad to say, many Christian girls are looking for exactly the same things in a guy that non-Christian girls are. It is the handsome, athletic, cool, smooth-talking, flirtatious guys who appeal to many Christian teenage girls. How many girls can look past a shy or plain exterior and see a heart that is wholly devoted to the Lord? Girls, you will find that these guys will make the best guys to date because the Lord can be the center of the relationship.

Guys, you sometimes need to take a risk also. So many guys refuse to date unless they can date the prettiest, sexiest girl at school. Instead of doing that, why don't you take out a girl who may not be so beautiful but who really loves the Lord? You may discover that she gets a lot prettier once you get to know her.

Do take the Christian girls out! You have a responsibility to date your Christian sisters. They have social needs, and they get tired of sitting home every weekend.

What To Do on a Date

The only limitation to things to do on dates is your creativity. Try to be imaginative and widely vary what you do on dates. Below is a list of some suggestions that have been given to me by students.[1]

Go to a:

rodeo	baseball game
circus	football game

1. Some of these suggestions also come from Howard Hendricks, *Heaven Help the Home,* pp. 101, 102.

basketball game
soccer game
hockey game
concert
fair

sidewalk art show
air show
zoo
museum or art gallery

Or go:

bowling
water skiing
cross country skiing
miniature golfing
fishing
sailing
roller skating
ice skating

jogging
hiking in mountains
canoeing or rafting
bike riding
play tennis
throw frisbee
play touch football
fly kites

Or:

study Bible together
visit a park
explore a new town
eat at a nice restaurant
make homemade
   ice cream
go on a picnic
take parents out

wash car (have
   water fight)
listen to music and talk
watch TV and
   eat popcorn
walk through cemetery and
   read markers
cook together

Discussion Questions

1. Read Judges 13—16. What is your impression of Samson? Describe his character in one phrase.

2. Judges 13:5 says that Samson was to be a Nazarite. What does this mean?

3. How do you reconcile the incident in Judges 14:1–4

with the fact that God had commanded the Jews not to
marry non-Jews? (see Deut. 7:3, 4)

4. Why do you think Samson wanted to marry this woman?

5. Who were the three women in Samson's life? Do you
think there were more? Why, or why not?

6. Describe the sort of women that Samson was attracted
to.

7. Why do you think God forsook Samson and allowed him
to be captured and to have his eyes put out?

8. How does this passage apply to your own life?

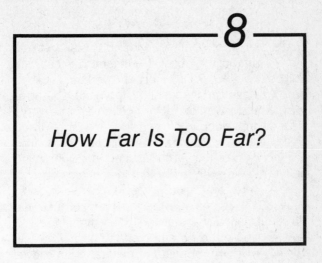

8

How Far Is Too Far?

We live in a sex-crazy world. This isn't something that I have to prove . . . just look around you. You turn on the television and see or hear sex hinted at. You go to the movies and see it explicitly. You turn on the radio and a great number of the songs suggest sex. Many legitimate magazines are becoming almost pornographic. *Time* magazine has been called by some "The Christians' *Playboy*" because of the almost weekly nude pictures. Television advertisers overtly appeal to our sex drives in order to get us to buy their products. We've all seen the commercial of the toothpaste with "sex appeal" or the shaving cream commercial where the lady croons, "Take it off, take it all off." Everywhere we turn we are surrounded by propaganda that encourages sexual looseness. How can a Christian single live in this sex jungle?

Be a Moral Light

God's desire for us is that we might stand out as moral lights in the midst of immoral darkness. In Philippians 2:15, Paul writes, "Prove yourselves to be blameless and innocent, children of God above reproach in the midst of a crooked and perverse generation, among whom you appear as lights in the world." Again, in Matthew 5:14, 16, Jesus said, "You are the light of the world.... Let your light shine before men in such a way that they might see your good works, and glorify your Father who is in heaven." God's design is that the quality of our moral life should be so high that it will cause unbelievers to take notice and to be attracted to Christ. There is nothing that will impress an immoral non-believer more than a believer who refuses to compromise the moral standards that he learns from in the Bible.

Keeping this in mind, God gives some guidelines to the Christian to govern his relationships with the opposite sex. Scripture does not explicitly answer the question, "How far is too far?" It does not say that kissing is wrong and holding hands is OK. It does, however, present some clear principles, and on the basis of these principles we have the responsibility for setting our moral standards.

Save Sexual Intercourse for Marriage

The Bible clearly teaches that it is wrong to "go all the way." Every time the Bible uses the word *fornication* it refers to premarital sexual intercourse (I Thess. 4:3; Eph. 5:3; I Cor. 6:13, 18; Acts 15:20; Heb. 13:4).

God's design is that sex is to be *only* for the marriage relationship. Sex is much like a fire. The same fire that warms a house can burn it down. What would happen if I took a burning log out of my fireplace and used it to build a fire on the living room rug? What would happen? I'd burn the house down! A fire in the fireplace gives warmth and comfort. But a fire burning outside the limits of the fireplace destroys and kills. The proper place for sex to burn, according to God, is in the fireplace of the marriage relationship. There it is good and gives warmth to the relationship. Apart from the marriage relationship, however, sex destroys and kills.

You Have Gone Too Far When Your Conscience Condemns You

As believers, we have the Holy Spirit living within us. One of the ministries of the Holy Spirit is to convict us of sin through our conscience. We need to be very sensitive to this conviction and to obey it instantly. If you feel that something is wrong and you violate your conscience and do it anyway, then the Bible teaches that to you it is sin (Rom. 14:14, 22, 23; I John 3:21).

Unfortunately, a person's conscience can become hardened. Do you remember when you were a kid and went barefoot during the summer? At the beginning of the summer your feet were very tender and it hurt to walk some places. But by the end of the summer your feet had become hardened and you could even walk over gravel without feeling it. Our hearts are this way. The longer we ignore the conviction of the Holy Spirit in our lives, the more hardened our hearts become to Him (Titus 1:15). This is very serious, because we have cut ourselves off from being able to hear what God wants us to do. A way to test yourself in this matter is to ask, "Do I have the same moral convictions that I had two years ago?" If your moral standards have weakened, then you need to go to God in repentance and ask Him to help you to reestablish your standards according to His Word.

You Have Gone Too Far When You Overly Arouse Sexual Passions

In I Corinthians 7:1, Paul says that it is wrong for a man to touch a woman so as to arouse sexual passions. In I Thessalonians 4:4, 5, Paul says that a man should control his sexual passions and desires. Once a guy and a girl begin petting, and excite their sexual desires in a way that they cannot lawfully and legitimately fulfill, then they have gone too far.

When your hormones instead of your better judgment start controlling your actions, then you have gone too far. This point is different in different people. Some people have serious problems just holding hands. Almost all guys, however, have problems after prolonged kissing. Of course, some arousal is normal and should not be worried about too much. But if it becomes so strong that it rules your actions, then it is sin.

There is one factor that enters here that we need to consider. God has designed a natural physical progression which culminates in sexual intercourse.

Holding hands leads to embracing which leads to kissing which leads to caressing which leads to intercourse. Once this progression is started, it is difficult for some people to stop, and when it is stopped it results in frustration. Also, after a while the thing that once thrilled and satisfied doesn't do so any more. We become more and more involved physically in order to gain satisfaction.

You Have Gone Too Far When Nudity Is Involved

Leviticus 20 teaches that uncovering the nakedness of another is sin. Any removal of clothes or caressing under the clothes is wrong.

The Consequences of Premarital Physical Intimacy

Some time ago I saw a bumper sticker that said, "If it feels good, do it." This is the way many young people view sex. A song I heard on the radio has a line that asks, "How can it be so wrong when it feels so right?" Many young people feel that it is wrong to place restrictions on love. They want to be free to do as they wish. It is true that we are free to do as we wish, but *we are not free to escape the consequences*.

Imagine a man learning to skydive. Just before the plane gets to the jump area he starts taking off his parachute. The instructor demands "What are you doing?" The skydiver replies, "I want to be free! I want to experience the freedom of soaring with no strings attached." The man would be a fool to jump without the parachute. He is free to do as he wishes and to jump without any strings attached but he is not free to escape the consequences.

Sex is like that. We are free to do as we wish. But we are not free to escape the consequences. There *will be* certain consequences of our actions. Proverbs 6:27–29 says, "Can a man take fire in his bosom, and his clothes not be burned? Or can a man walk on hot coals, and his feet not be scorched? So is the one who goes in to his neighbor's wife; whoever touches her will not go unpunished." Sex is a fire! You can't play with it and not be burned!

What, then, are some of the consequences that result from intimate physical relationships before marriage?

It Will Take Away the Peace of Your Soul

Peter writes in I Peter 2:11, "Beloved, I urge you . . . to abstain from fleshly lusts, which wage war against the soul." War is the absence of peace, and that is exactly what you will experience when you become involved in an immoral relationship. You will experience guilt, conviction, uneasiness, and unhappiness.

Someone once said, "We don't break God's laws, they break us." There is a great deal of truth in that statement. Proverbs 6:32 says, "The one who commits adultery with a woman is lacking sense; he who would destroy himself does it." Moral impurity destroys us emotionally. Those who become slaves to their passions have so much inner turmoil that it can literally drive them to a nervous breakdown or even to suicide.

It Will Damage Your Relationship with God

Sin drives a wedge between us and God. Isaiah 59:2 says, "Your iniquities have made a separation between you and your God, and your sins have hid His face from you."

Sexual sin will cause a person to lose his desire for spiritual things. Jesus said that "everyone who does evil hates the light, and does not come to the light, lest his deeds be exposed" (John 3:20). Everything that has to do with God, such as prayer, Bible study, witnessing, and strong Spirit-filled preaching exposes our sins and brings guilt, and so we begin to shun such things. And after a while, even though you know that what you are doing is wrong, you don't care. You have become enslaved to your passions (II Peter 2:18, 19). Apart from the grace of God at this point it is impossible to repent and come back to Him.

It Will Damage Your Usefulness to God

Paul teaches us in II Timothy 2:21 that God will not use a dirty vessel. Only a man who is cleansed from immorality will be a sanctified vessel of honor useful to the Master. I think this passage teaches that God puts a man on the shelf, at least temporarily, while he is involved in sexual impurity. This does not mean that he can't continue doing "religious work" but it does mean that God temporarily withdraws His hand of blessing from that person's life while he is involved in that sin. Recently I saw a sign in a local department store that read, "Merchandise slightly soiled. Greatly reduced in value." That is what happens to us when we become involved in sexual sin.

Also, if your sin becomes public, it will hurt your testimony for the Lord. Even if you repent and get right with God; your testimony is still hurt. People are much slower to forgive and to forget than God is. They will not soon forget your immorality, and the voice of your past behavior may drown out your present words.

If your sin becomes public, it may cause others to stumble and may cause the name of the Lord to be dishonored. Non-Christians may look at your life and say, "If that is the way a Christian acts, then there must not be much to Christianity. It must be fake." And so that person may be lost for eternity because of your bad witness. It will also give others an excuse for blaspheming God and saying that there is no God.

There is an interesting illustration of this in II Samuel 12. David committed adultery with Bathsheba, and had her husband Uriah murdered. In II Samuel 12 the prophet Nathan confronted King David with his sin and said, "By this deed you have given occasion to the enemies of the Lord to blaspheme." David had given a strong testimony of the Lord to the surrounding nations, but when the news of his adultery spread, it gave his enemies ammunition to ridicule the God of Israel. Needless to say, God is very concerned that His servants walk worthy of His name, the name by which they have been called (Col. 1:10).

It May Damage Your Relationship with Each Other

Often, two lovers in the heat of passion think that physical involvement will draw them closer and cement their relationship. This is true in marriage, but before marriage physical involvement may actually drive couples *apart* spiritually and emotionally. It may do this in several ways.

First, it may lead to a breakdown of communication. You are great lovers on the couch after her parents have gone to bed but you can't really talk to one another any more. All you want to do when you are alone is to be involved physically. Petting is habit-forming and often overshadows every other area of the relationship.

Second, it may cause mistrust. The guy may think, "If she'll do this with me, who else has she done it with?" The girl may think, "If he does this with me, who else has he done it with?" And so a seed of mistrust is sown that may cause problems later.

Third, it may lead to a loss of respect. The more you get involved physically, the more you will lose your self-respect and also your respect for the other person. You feel guilty and dirty and unhappy with yourself over your lack of moral strength and you disrespect the other person for his or her lack of moral strength.

Fourth, it may lead to dishonesty. Girls, let me tell you something about guys. A guy, once he has become aroused sexually, will tell you almost anything to get you to lower your moral standards. If the only time your boy friend tells you that he loves you is when you are physically involved with one another, then I would strongly suspect his real intentions. Guys will sometimes just use the phrase, "I love you" in order to seduce a girl.

Fifth, it may lead to bitterness. You may secretly become bitter toward the other person for causing you to violate your own moral standards. You blame your boy friend or girlfriend for what has happened and so become secretly bitter toward him or her.

Finally, it will lead to loss of spiritual fellowship with one another. You will not be able to talk to one another about spiritual things anymore. Your relationship may be on the physical and emotional level but not on the spiritual level. This obviously leads to an incomplete relationship.

It May Cause Problems When You Marry

Our present is vitally affected by our past. Bill Gothard, in his Institute of Basic Youth Conflicts, gives example after example of married couples who have problems because of premarital moral impurity. It can cause mistrust, communication breakdowns, loss of respect, and bitterness later when you marry. Also, those who engage in premarital sex are most likely to engage in extramarital sex later.

I am not saying that you can't have a happy and successful marriage if you are involved in premarital sexual impurity, but I am saying that it increases the probability of problems later. The question is, Are you willing to risk your future by being impure now?

You Risk Pregnancy and Veneral Disease

I'm sure that you have been reminded of these things many times. Premarital pregnancy is on the rise despite the free availability of contraceptives. The statistics are staggering. One out of every six teenage girls becomes pregnant without being married. In 1974, teenagers accounted for approximately one in five births—about 617,000 babies, plus a quarter of a million abortions.[1]

Some time ago, Anson Mount, *Playboy* magazine's representive to the college campus, was asked this question by a student. "Mr. Mount, for five years I have read *Playboy,* I've dressed *Playboy,* I've lived *Playboy,* I've been a real *Playboy* cat. But now I've got a question. I want to know what the *Playboy* cat is supposed to do when his kitty's going to have kittens." Mr. Mount's reply was, "I'm afraid we don't have the answer to everything. You'll have to see an obstetrician about that one."[2] No matter what you do to try to prevent it, pregnancy is a very real threat when you toy around with premarital sex.

1. Theodore Litz, *The Person,* p. 367.
2. John Bisagno, *The Power of Positive Preaching to the Saved,* p. 86, 87.

You Will Bring the Judgment of God on You

In I Thessalonians 4:6, Paul solemnly warns the Thessalonians not to become involved in sexual immorality, because God would judge it. God sees it as a sin that causes you not only to violate yourself but also to violate another person. "Do not be deceived, God is not mocked; for whatever a man sows, this he will also reap" (Gal. 6:7). God *always* judges sin. Perhaps He may judge it in some of the ways that we have just listed. Perhaps He may judge it in an extreme, unexpected way, as He judged David for his adultery with Bathsheba. In that instance the child died. God judged Amnon for raping his sister—his brother murdered him. Fortunately, however, God in His grace rarely judges today in such extreme ways. But do not deceive yourself; He still does judge.

Conclusion

I think that the issues discussed in this chapter are issues we should consider very seriously. Sexual immorality can literally destroy us and our partner. We need to never forget that our date today will be somebody else's mate tomorrow. Do you want to marry someone who has already made love to someone else? Of course not! Neither does someone else want to marry you if you have already given all of yourself to someone else. Love, of course, is willing to forget the past, but why have a past that needs forgetting? Right now ask God to help you keep yourself and those whom you date pure for the mate that God has for both of you.

We tend to think that we can hide our past sins from God and from others. But this is foolishness. We can't hide our sexual sins from God in the bedroom or in the dark. Secret sin on earth is open scandal in heaven. Neither can we usually hide our sexual sin from others. Sexual sin has a strange way of coming to the light. For these reasons we need to guard our actions diligently.

Discussion Questions

1. Read I Thessalonians 4:1–8. According to v. 3, what is the will of God for your life?

2. In v. 6, what do you think it means to "transgress or defraud" (NASB)?

3. What does Paul say will happen if we "transgress or defraud" someone? What do you think this means?

4. Read Genesis 39:1–23. Do you think Joseph was lonely? Why, or why not?

5. Why do you think that God allowed this to happen to Joseph?

6. How did Joseph react when he was faced with temptation? Why did he refuse Potiphar's wife? (see vv. 9, 12, compare with II Tim. 2:22 and I Cor. 6:18). What does this say about how we should react to sexual temptation? Be specific.

9

How to Keep From Going Too Far

In Romans 13:11–14, Paul gives some pointed exhortations to the Roman believers who lived in an unbelievably immoral and degenerate society. He exhorted them to lay aside deeds of darkness and to put on the armor of light. They were not to be involved in carousing, drunkenness sexual promiscuity, sensuality, strife, and jealousy, but instead were to walk in a godly manner. He concluded his exhortation by saying, "Put on the Lord Jesus Christ, and make no provision for the flesh in regard to its lusts." The "flesh" is that part of us that desires to disobey God. One of the key areas in our lives that the flesh desires to rule is in our sex lives. Will we obey the flesh, or will we obey God?

Preserving Sexual Purity

There are some practical things that we as Christians can do in order to avoid allowing ourselves into situations in which the temptation to sexual impurity is too great too overcome. The Lord promises in I Corinthians 10:13 that He will not allow us to be tempted past what we are able to stand. This promise, however, does not apply when we foolishly make provision for the flesh and allow ourselves to get into situations that we can't handle. What, then, are some of the things that we can do in order not to "make provision for the flesh"?

Walk by the Spirit

The most important thing that a Christian young person needs to do in order to insure sexual purity is to walk by the Spirit. There is a wonderful promise found in Galatians 5:16, where we read, "Walk by the Spirit, and you will not carry out the desire of the flesh." It is the flesh within us that desires to disobey God's moral law. We have no power on our own to resist the urgings of the flesh, but by the power of the indwelling Spirit, we are able to resist. We need to be careful to walk by the Spirit, otherwise we are wide open to temptation and are defenseless against the power of sin.

Walking by the Spirit means that you have a vital and alive spiritual life. You are yielded to the absolute and utter control of the Holy Spirit. You have a consistent devotional life and your heart is warm toward the things of God.

But this sort of spiritual life takes cultivation. Just as a beautiful garden requires constant care and cultivation, so also a vital spiritual life requires constant cultivation. This cultivation includes Bible study, prayer, evangelism, and church work.

When you are walking by the Spirit, your greatest desire is to please the Lord in your life. Only when you have a deep desire to please God will you have the strength to resist temptation. This is because desire is only overcome by higher desire. Passion is only overcome by higher passion. Only when our passion to please God is greater than our sexual passion will we have the power to overcome temptation in the day of testing.

Keep in the Word

Closely related to walking in the Spirit is Bible study. A central theme of the Book of Proverbs is that gaining wisdom, knowledge, and understanding of God's Word will keep a person from sexual sin. We read in Proverbs 7:1–5:

> My son, keep my words,
> And treasure my commandments within you.
> Keep my commandments and live,
> And my teaching as the apple of your eye.
> Bind them on your fingers;
> Write them on the tablet of your heart.
> Say to wisdom, "You are my sister,"
> And call understanding your intimate friend;
> That they may keep you from an adulteress,
> From the foreigner who flatters with her words.

David gives a similar thought in Psalm 119:11 when he says, "Thy word I have treasured in my heart, that I may not sin against Thee." This does not mean that Bible knowledge is a magic formula to protect us from sin. Hearing the Word of God is meaningless without obeying it. But "treasuring" the Word of God in our hearts, incorporating it into our thoughts, does give us strength against temptation.

Set a Standard

You need to decide what your moral standard will be *before* you are in the place of temptation. It is much easier to break no standard than it is to break some standard. Don't just slide; decide! A standard is much like a military line of defense. You commit yourself to preventing the enemy from penetrating that line of defense (Job. 31:1).

A word of warning is in line here—especially to girls. Be prepared for an angry response from the guy when he tries to violate your standard and you stop him. The reason for this is that when a guy has become aroused sexually, it frustrates him to stop. He expresses his frustration by becoming angry at you. If, however, he persists, and keeps trying to break your standard, then tell him to go take a long walk on a short pier. He isn't interested in you as a person; all he is interested in is your body as a tool to gratify his lust. If you stick to your standard, however, he'll respect you for it. He may be angry at first, but once he cools down he will respect you.

Girls, determine to reserve your body for your husband-to-be. Let no man handle you wrongly—

because you are reserved for one very special man. On your wedding night, you want to look into your lawful husband's eyes and with a clear conscience and a pure heart say, "Here I am, pure and ready, God's gift to you, a virgin." This is God's will for you (I Thess. 4:3). God says in Hebrews 13:4, "Let the marriage bed be undefiled." This means that you are to come to the marriage bed as a virgin. Guys, this applies to you also!

What Are Your Motives?

Examine your motives for going out with the person you are dating. Are your motives pure? In chapter 1 we looked at some purposes for dating. Do these purposes line up with your motives? It is very possible to date from impure motives. A girl may just be using a guy to make some other guy jealous. Or a guy may date a girl only in order to see how far she will let him go physically. We need to examine our motives for wanting to date, for none of us are above dating for wrong motives.

Beware of Dating Someone with Low Moral Standards

Dating a person with low moral standards may be too great a temptation to you. If a guy knows that a girl has low moral standards, he is even more tempted to become involved physically. In the Book of Proverbs young men are constantly warned to avoid being around morally loose women because they may entice to sin (Prov. 6:20-29; 5:8; 7:25). Ideally, the guy should have full control of his passions, but actually it often takes both the guy and the girl to keep the physical area under control. Sometimes the girl must be the "stopper." I believe that the best policy then is to date only people that you highly respect as Christians.

Discuss It and Pray About It

Make a point of seeking to keep the relationship centered on God. I recommend that you discuss openly with one another the problems that you might have and how you might help one another. But don't be too explicit in sharing physical problems, for this may tempt you even more. I suggest that you plan to close each date with prayer. This will help regulate your actions on dates.

See One Another as Brother and Sister in Christ

In I Timothy 5:1, 2, Paul tells Timothy to look at the younger men as brothers and on the younger women as sisters. Girls, you should see your boy friend first as a brother in Christ, and only secondly as your boy friend. Likewise, guys, you need to see your girlfriend first as a sister in the Lord and only secondly as your girlfriend. The way we look at someone affects the way we treat them.

Beware of Tempting Situations

Don't allow yourself into situations that might present strong temptations. If you are on a diet, it is not wise to stand around in the kitchen when your mom is cooking. Likewise, if you are easily tempted into sexual sin, then you need to avoid situations that might tempt you—such as being alone on the couch watching TV after your parents have gone to bed, or going parking, or to secluded places. Another thing that might help is to impose upon yourselves a ten o'clock curfew. A friend of mine shared that this really helped him.

The Bible says, "Make no provision for the flesh," and "flee fornication." I saw an illustration of this in the newspaper recently. Senator George McGovern was at a party in Washington when he noticed a beautiful blonde in a low-cut dress giving him the eye. He remarked to a friend, "That looks like a sex scandal waiting to happen! I'm getting out of here." He left immediately.

It is interesting to note that Senator McGovern exactly followed the biblical formula for escaping sexual sin. I Corinthians 6:18 says to "flee fornication." Run from it. Don't try to fight it. Joseph in the Old Testament fled when Potiphar's wife tried to seduce him. You can imagine what would have happened if Joseph had said to Potiphar's wife, "Let's sit down on the couch over here and rationally talk this over."

The principle is clear. Don't allow yourself to get into a tempting situation. If you do, you're asking for trouble.

Dress Modestly

In I Timothy 2:9, Paul says, "I want women to adorn themselves with proper clothing, modestly and discreetly. . . ." The reason this is so important is that guys are sexually aroused by sight. Many girls just don't seem to realize this. Girls, on the other hand, are turned on primarily by thought and touch. Girls need to understand that certain types of dress really cause guys problems. Tight blouses, tight slacks, halters, no bras, and skimpy bathing suits are all immodest. Any kind of dress that accents the sexual aspects of a woman is immodest. If a girl just uses a little common sense, she can dress very modestly. Bill Gothard suggests that a girl dress to draw attention to her face, not her body. Often a girl will dress to emphasize her body when she feels that her personality will not attract guys. There is something wrong when a girl thinks that the only way that she can attract guys is with her body.

I saw a perfect illustration of this some time ago, when I taught at a high school youth camp. Almost all the girls dressed very modestly except for one girl, Ruth. She was an extremely beautiful girl but had a physical defect. After I had taught the subject of accepting ourselves the way God made us, Ruth came up to talk to me. She revealed that she was very insecure and felt ugly because of her physical defect. She also confessed that she had had some real problems with petting and sex. I then began to understand. She felt ugly and insecure because of her physical defect, and thought that the only way she could attract guys was with her body. We had a good talk, and I think she started to accept herself the way God made her.

One thing to remember when we talk about this issue of dressing modestly is the teaching of I Corinthians 8:12. If we cause a person with a weak conscience to sin, we have sinned against God. This is a very serious thing, and girls should realize that it is very possible for them to cause guys to sin by their dress.

Sometimes girls excuse their choice of clothes by saying, "It's just the style. I'll look like an old maid if I dress any other way." We need to remember, however, that the Bible warns us against copying the behavior and customs of this world when they run contrary to the Word of God (Rom. 12:2).

By the way, guys, you can usually tell a girl's sexual morals by the way she dresses. Proverbs 7:10 says that you can tell a harlot by her attire. And almost 4,000 years ago, Judah, son of Jacob, could tell a woman was a harlot by the way she dressed (Gen. 38:13–19).

These nine suggestions are not, of course, complete. As you struggle with this problem, I'm sure that you will discover other things that need to be added to this list.

Are You a Wall or a Door?

In Song of Solomon 8:8, 9, we see that Solomon and his wife, the Shulammite, are recalling the days of her youth. Evidently, the Shulammite's father died very early in her life and so her brothers looked after her. When she reached sexual maturity, her brothers had a conference to decide how to preserve her sexual purity. "We have a little sister, and she has no breasts [i.e., she is still sexually immature]; What shall we do for our sister on the day when she is spoken for?" They decide, "If she is a wall, we shall build on her a battlement of silver; But if she is a door, we shall barricade her with planks of cedar."

What is all this about walls and doors? The answer is simple. By a wall the brothers meant one who resisted premarital sexual involvement. When men would try to violate her standard, she resisted them like a wall. She was immovable and strong. The Shulammite says in 8:10 that she was a wall until she met and married Solomon, her husband. Verse 9 says that if their sister were a wall, the brothers would build on her a battlement of silver. That means that they would honor her. It is interesting to see just how honored the Shulammite became because she remained sexually pure. She became queen to the most powerful king Israel ever had and was the object of the greatest love poem ever written, the Song of Solomon! I am not saying that you will become a queen and have great poems written about you if you remain sexually pure until you marry, but I am saying that if you remain sexually pure you will be honored, not only by God but also by man.

The alternative to being a wall is being a door. To be a door means to be one who yields easily to sexual involvement to all who desire to open her door. The Shulammite's brothers decided that if she were a door then they would barricade her with planks of cedar. This means that they would have to take precautionary measures to defend her so that she would not suffer for her moral weakness and be sexually violated. They would have to limit and restrict her freedom.

Of course the obvious question is, Are you a wall or a door? Why don't you bow your head right now and ask God to give you the strength to be a wall. Though this figure of speech is specifically applied to a girl in Song of Solomon, I believe it can also apply to a guy.

How Can I Remain a Wall?

As you face several more years before you get married, perhaps you are wondering, "How can I hold out? How can I stay sexually pure? The temptation is too great." Be of good cheer; I have good news for you. I think that if we will seek the Lord first in our lives then God gives us some amazing promises concerning temptation. God says in I Corinthians 10:13 that He will not allow us to be tempted beyond what we are able, but will instead provide a way of escape from the temptation. Every temptation that comes our way is filtered by the Father so that it is not too great for us to resist. Isn't that a tremendous thought?

Another verse that I love is Psalm 34:7, where the psalmist says that "the angel of the Lord encamps around those who fear Him." The Lord puts a wall of protection around us (perhaps a wall of angels!) and guards us from temptations that we can't handle. I've seen this many times in my life, and I'm sure you have too, when the Lord has amazingly and miraculously kept us out of situations that could have morally destroyed us. It is as if we walk on the edge of a cliff above a bottomless chasm; it is only the marvelous grace of our Lord that prevents us from falling. "Now to Him who is able to keep you from stumbling, and to make you stand in the presence of His glory blame-less with great joy, to the only God our Savior, through Jesus Christ our Lord, be glory, majesty, dominion and authority, before all time and now and forever. Amen" (Jude 24, 25).

What If I Have Already Blown It?

Perhaps you are thinking, "I'd like to be a wall, but I have already been a door in the past." If so, then don't despair! God tells us in I John 1:9 that "if we confess our sins, He is faithful and righteous to forgive us our sins and to cleanse us from all unrigh-teousness." If we are willing to come to God and confess, repent, and turn from our sin, then He is willing and able to forgive us and forget our sin.

But sometimes it is more difficult for us to forgive ourselves than it is for God to forgive us. Some people spend a lifetime worrying over past mistakes. One of Satan's favorite tricks is to enslave us with our past—to tell us that after what we have done, God will never use us again. Satan will tell us to give up and to give in because we aren't able to fight this sin. With Satan's help, our past sins and the accompany-ing guilt become a relentless bloodhound that won't stop chasing us.

The apostle Paul had a sin such as this in his life that Satan could have used in this way. Paul was partially responsible for the murder of Stephen (see Acts 6:8—8:3). How did Paul handle his past sin and guilt? Did he allow Satan to keep on accusing him and enslaving him with it? No! In Philippians 3:13, 14 he says, "Brethren, I do not regard myself as having laid hold of it [perfection] yet; but one thing I do: forgetting what lies behind and reaching forward to what lies ahead, I press on. . . ." Paul is saying that if we have sin in our past, then we simply need to confess it and get right with God and then, by God's help, to forget it.

Conclusion

As we conclude these two chapters on physical relationships in dating, let me be very honest with you. Keeping a serious dating relationship morally pure is not easy. The more you care for one another the greater the temptations will be to become involved physically. I wish I could tell you that it will be easy, but I can't. It will be a struggle. I *can* tell you that it will be worth it if you wait. Rest assured, God always honors obedience.

I suggest that you bow your head right now and ask God to give you the strength through the power of the Holy Spirit to remain morally pure. If you have already violated His standard, then ask God to forgive you and to give you the power not to do it again. Remember, "Walk by the Spirit, and you will not carry out the desire of the flesh" (Gal. 5:16).

Discussion Questions

1. Read II Samuel 11:1—12:5. Acts 13:22 says that David was a man after God's own heart, and yet David committed the terrible sin of adultery. How is it possible for a spiritual person to commit such an evil deed?

2. At what point in 11:2–4 did David sin? (see James 1:14, 15). Comment on the difference between temptation and sin.

3. Over a year passed between the sin of chapter 11 and Nathan's reproof in chapter 12. What sort of year do you think it was for David emotionally and spiritually? (see Ps. 32:3, 4)

4. Read 12:13, 14. Do you feel God is too easy on David? Why, or why not?

5. At what point did God forgive David?

6. Is David's confession in II Samuel 12:13 genuine? How do you know? (see Ps. 51).

7. In II Samuel 12:14, what does Nathan mean when he says, "By this deed you have given occasion to the enemies of the Lord to blaspheme"?

8. If God forgave David, then why did the child die? (12:14–20).

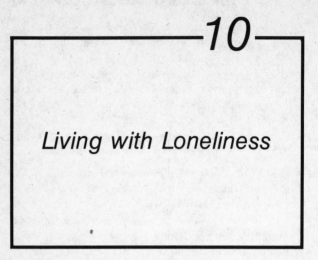

10

Living with Loneliness

Some time ago I watched the Charlie Brown Valentine Special on television. One scene that made a deep impression on me was the one at the school valentine party. All the students brought valentines to school and then put them all in a brightly decorated box. During the party the box was shaken up and one of the students (the teacher's pet) began to give out the valentines. Charlie Brown sat at his desk patiently waiting to get some valentines—but they never came. Everybody got valentines but Charlie Brown. When I saw Charlie Brown sitting lonely and dejected at this desk, I felt a sad emptiness. That is loneliness! It is a feeling of not being loved and cared for by others. It is perhaps the most despairing emotion that a person can feel.

Loneliness is widespread today, especially among teenagers. One survey conducted by the Purdue Public Opinion Poll reveals loneliness to be the biggest problem confronting teenagers today.

What Is Loneliness?

Loneliness, first and foremost, is a *feeling.* Being alone is physical, but being lonely is psychological. Aloneness does not necessarily mean loneliness. Thoreau at Walden Pond was alone, but he was not lonely. Aloneness can lead to loneliness, as Defoe's Robinson Crusoe discovered before he found a companion in Friday.

Loneliness is, basically, a feeling that you aren't loved and are not important to others. It is a feeling that nobody cares and that nobody needs you. Often it is centered on one other person who doesn't seem to care and love you the way you need to be cared for and loved. Loneliness usually manifests itself in a depressed, lifeless, and empty feeling.

Many different things can cause loneliness. Boredom, being alone too long, seeing friends date and get married, special occasions, weariness, sickness, breakups, discouragement, parties, and reminiscing about former love relationships are all things that can lead to loneliness.

Perhaps the primary time young singles feel lonely is when they see others who are dating and having a good time. A young person sitting home alone will cry out in prayer, "God, why don't you give me a boy friend or a girlfriend *now*?"

There are two types of loneliness. There is a loneliness in the will of God and then there is a loneliness out of the will of God. There is a misconception that *all* loneliness is bad. True, loneliness is often our own fault and comes because we are self-centered and wallow in self-pity. As long as we are more interested in ourselves than in others, we will feel lonely. But sometimes loneliness comes from God—as a gift! As Bruce Larson says, "Loneliness is basically a gift. It is a reminder of our humanity. It is the thing that continually drives us to a relationship with God and our neighbor. To take away loneliness would remove the constant motivation to live in fellowship with God and the saints and with our brothers in the world."[1]

In Scripture, we find that God allows His saints to go through periods of aloneness and loneliness to teach them to depend solely and utterly upon Him. We find David spending months and years alone on the hillsides with his sheep. We discover Joseph being uprooted from his home and family and thrust into the lonely life of a slave. Moses spent some forty years in the desert keeping sheep. There is some evidence that Paul spent three years alone in the desert. The prophet Elijah was a lonely wilderness wanderer, as was also John the Baptist. It was in those times of solitude and loneliness that God molded the character of these great saints.

When God wants to use a man, He will often put him through a discipline of loneliness as He did these

1. Bruce Larson, "The Gift of Loneliness, *Faith at Work,* Oct. 1974, p. 26.

great biblical saints. We often pray, "God, use me." But perhaps instead our prayer should be, "God, make me usable!" Spiritual maturity and qualification for service is often brought about by suffering. There are no short cuts to spirituality. Valleys of discouragement often come before the mountains of victory; pain before pleasure; hurt before honor; and crisis before Christ-likeness. Thus, one of the key purposes of loneliness is to crowd us to Christ and force us to faith. God is more concerned with our holiness than with our present happiness, and so the process of sanctification is often a very painful one. Part of God's program is loneliness. He will allow us to be alone and lonely in order to force us to turn to Him.

How To Deal with Loneliness

There is a right way and a wrong way to respond to loneliness. The following is an example of the wrong way to respond: You feel lonely and so you think "If I only had someone to love me, I wouldn't be lonely." The more you think about it, the more depressed you become, and this leads to anger. "Why don't you give me someone, God? You promise to meet my needs. I need someone." Or you may become angry at yourself. "If only I wasn't so dull and ugly!" But this just leads to guilt, because you know it's wrong to be angry. And so you become more depressed. Before you know it, you are caught in a vicious cycle.[2]

2. Marilyn McGinnis, *Single, The Woman's View*, p. 93.

How, then, should you respond when faced with loneliness? First, be honest with God and tell Him how you feel. Then, thank Him for your loneliness and recognize His purpose in allowing this to happen. Realize that you are not the only one who has ever felt lonely. Patiently accept this as God's will for you, without argument and without amendment. Remember, God allows loneliness in your life in order to crowd you closer to Him and to teach you greater dependence upon Him. He wants you to recognize that "the Lord alone is your portion."

Discussion Questions

1. Is loneliness always bad? Why or why not?
2. Name as many Bible characters as you can who went through periods of solitude.
3. Describe as completely as you can the way loneliness feels.
4. Study the Book of Ruth. What principles can you find that relate to loneliness and how a person should handle it?

11

Breaking Up Is Hard to Do...

I recently heard of a guy whose motto in dating was, "Rush 'em, mush 'em, crush 'em, then flush 'em." Many of us have, unfortunately, experienced the "crush 'em—flush 'em" stage.

One of the most painful times in a young person's life is during and immediately following a serious breakup. Almost everybody has had a bad breakup at some time or another when he or she was really hurt. Each time I speak on this subject I ask those in the audience who have had a bad breakup which really hurt them to raise their hands. There is always a very large percentage who raise their hands. To those who haven't yet had a bad breakup, I predict that they will probably have one eventually.

Problems that May Result from Breakups

Bad breakups can do serious damage to people—emotionally, spiritually, and even physically. We need to be aware of possible problems that may arise so that we won't be caught unaware and so that we will know how to deal with them when and if they come.

Damaged Self-Image

Often if your boy friend or girlfriend has broken up with you, you will turn inward and begin to think, "He (or she) doesn't like me because there is something wrong with me. I am a failure as a person." Thus when you need encouragement more than ever you instead become more insecure and discouraged. You may even begin to *expect* people not to like you and to reject you.

There is, of course, a place for healthy introspection. If you have been dropped by someone, you need to ask if perhaps you were selfish or inconsiderate. If that was the case, then you need to repent and ask God help you to work on those areas. A wise man is not someone who never makes mistakes, but a wise man is someone who learns from his mistakes and does not repeat them.

Introspection becomes unhealthy when you begin to focus on the past alone and to despair of improving your faults. Perhaps you were in the wrong in a certain relationship, but as the cliché goes, "You can't cry over spilt milk." Mop it up and work on not spilling it again.

Depression and Loneliness

After a bad breakup you may go into a deep depression. You have no energy and are basically miserable. The source of this depression is self-pity. You almost enjoy feeling sorry for yourself and you enjoy the sympathy you get from others. I remember one time I ruined a vacation for those around me by my depression over a bad breakup.

Obviously, there will be some depression after a serious breakup. This is natural and normal and is to be expected. But if it continues for a long time and does not get better, then something is wrong. You need to really examine your heart and ask, "Why is this depression lingering?" It might be good for you to share what is on your heart with someone you respect and to seek his or her encouragement and counsel. I would also suggest that you read the book, *Happiness Is a Choice,* by Meier and Minirth (Baker, 1978).

Deep Bitterness

When we feel that we have been treated unjustly, it is natural and human to feel bitter. I can remember that this was a serious problem for me several years ago when a girl I was dating unexpectedly broke up with me. She had "led me on" about her feelings for me and I had a deep affection for her. After the initial hurt, my reaction was anger and bitterness. For several months my bitterness toward her destroyed my prayer life and made me an unhappy and miserable person to be around. All my bitterness did was to hurt me even more.

Bitterness not only hurts a person emotionally, but it also hurts a person spiritually. Jesus said in Matthew 6:15 that if we don't forgive others, then God won't forgive us. This does not mean that we will not go to heaven but it does mean that an unforgiving and bitter spirit causes us to break fellowship with God. I can remember that while I was bitter in my heart toward this girl I did not want to pray or read my Bible. My heart was cold toward spiritual things.

Bitterness, though, as I am sure you know, is not an easy thing to overcome. It took me several months. Granted, the other person may have been in the wrong, but you still need to forgive that person in your heart. One practical thing that I found helped me was to pray for my former girlfriend every day that God would bless her and be with her. It really helped.

Mistrust of the Opposite Sex

A common reaction to a bad breakup is to think, "All guys are this way," or "All girls are this way, so why trust them?" Besides, after being dropped 2,539 times, who wouldn't begin to feel a little negative toward the opposite sex? And so you find yourself reluctant to become involved in another relationship or to trust someone again. Needless to say, this is a bad attitude. Fortunately, time (and another pretty girl or handsome guy) usually helps overcome this problem.

A Bad Witness to Others

Ron and Shirley are perhaps the classic example of how not to break up. They had been dating almost a year when Shirley flew in to visit Ron, who was a seminary student. During the week, Ron gave her an engagement ring. She then called home to tell her parents the good news. The next day, as Ron was putting her on the plane to go home, he got cold feet and asked her for the ring back. She literally went to pieces there at the airport and boarded the plane in tears. To my knowledge, they have not seen one another or talked to one another since.

The sad part about this story is that Ron had been witnessing to Shirley's non-Christian parents. How do you think they felt about Christianity after seeing the way this "preacher" treated their daughter?

Physical Problems

A girl I know was engaged to a young man some time ago when he unexpectedly dropped her. He didn't even break up with her in person but instead sent a "Dear Mary" letter. A short time later she developed a low blood sugar problem that will affect her the rest of her life. She told me that her doctor suggested that the emotional trauma of the broken engagement helped trigger the low blood sugar condition. The point is that our emotional health greatly affects our physical health. Bad breakups, as in this girl's case, can sometimes cause serious physical problems.

How To Gently Break Up with Someone

It is not wrong to break up with someone. This is a natural thing that is part of growing up and beginning to date. Also, no matter how you break up with someone, they will be hurt to some degree. There really is no "gentle" way to break up with someone, but there are some things that you can do to soften the hurt and to help prevent serious problems from developing.

Seek Counsel

It is always wise to seek the counsel of those whom you respect before you make important decisions. Often we do things when we are emotionally upset that we are sorry for later. Many times people have broken up in the heat of a fight or a misunderstanding only to be sorry for it later. In the Book of Proverbs we are often warned to seek the counsel of others (Prov. 13:10; 19:20; 11:14). Go to a friend that you trust and respect, explain the situation, and then ask his advice.

Give Warning

Sometimes this is very difficult to do but it makes it easier for the person that you break up with—it gives them a chance to prepare themselves emotionally. An abrupt breakup is like the sudden death of a close relative. It is easier to prepare yourself emotionally for the death of a relative whom you know is dying than it is to face an unexpected, sudden death.

If you are dissatisfied with the relationship, don't hide it. Avoid—at all costs—leading someone on. It is cruel and dishonest to say something either verbally or physically and not to mean it in your heart. Make a conscious point of saying only what you really feel and of not leading the person on.

If you are dissatisfied with the relationship then you might casually drop hints about how you feel. For instance, you might say, "Things haven't been going too well in our relationship lately. Maybe we need to take some time to rethink things." Perhaps it might be well to suggest that you not see one another for a week prior to the final break in order to give one another time to think through the relationship.

This suggestion is not a hard and fast rule, and of course each situation must be handled differently, but it might prove helpful in some cases.

Be Supportive

When you do break up, try to add as many ego builders and compliments as you can. Tell the person you're breaking up with how much you have enjoyed the relationship and how it has helped you. Don't be all negative when you break up with someone.

Don't Back Out

Once you have made up your mind that breaking up is the right thing to do, then don't back out of it or let the other person talk you out of going through with it. To put it off and to have to do it again makes it even harder on both parties. It is like stabbing a person with a knife and then twisting it.

Be Honest and Give Reasons Why

When you break up with someone, don't just say, "God has led me to do this." That is a cop-out. After all, how can anyone argue with God? I don't think that we should bring God into it unless we have *seriously* sought God's will by much prayer (and even, sometimes, fasting).

I think that you have a responsibility to the other person to tell him or her *why* you want to break up. Give some good reasons. It may hurt, but in the long run it probably will prove helpful. I've asked many audiences of young people this question and almost all of them have agreed that they would like to be told why when someone breaks up with them, even though it might hurt.

Pray

This is very important. Commit yourself to pray for the person that you break up with, that he or she can take it well and get over it quickly without serious emotional or physical problems developing. After all, since you caused the hurt, you have a responsibility to pray for him or her to get over the hurt.

How To Respond When Someone Breaks Up with You

Whether or not you like it, the chances are very good that at some time in your future you will experience a bad breakup. How do you respond when someone that you care for deeply breaks up with you and says that he or she is not interested in a romantic relationship with you?

Before we look at the spiritual side of this problem, let us look at the psychological response to deep grief. Psychologists have discovered a very predictable process that people go through when they experience intense grief. This process applies to all types of grief, including the loss of a loved one to death, divorce, and a serious breakup. First comes what is called *denial.* The person is unwilling to accept that this has happened to them. The second stage is *anger turned outward.* The grieved person becomes angry at those who hurt him and also at God. The third stage is called *anger turned inward.* The grieved person becomes angry at himself and blames himself for what has happened. He may also feel guilty. The fourth stage in the process is called *genuine grief.* This is when the full force of the tragedy hits the grieved person and he hurts the most. This stage is characterized by weeping. The final stage in the process of grief is called the *resolution stage.* The grieved person is finally able to deal with his grief and to resolve it.

Understanding these fives stages of grief will in no way prevent them from happening. These stages almost always occur. Understanding these stages, however, may help a person to go through them more easily and not to become trapped in one of the stages, which would lead to depression.

The Bible teaches that God has a purpose for allowing hurts into our lives. Perhaps He wants us to become more sensitive to the needs and hurts of others. Or perhaps He wants to destroy our self-sufficiency and to force us to lean on and depend on Him completely. Just as people usually don't come to a doctor unless they are bleeding, so also we often don't come to God unless we are hurting. But whatever the reason that God has allowed this to happen, even if we don't know what it is, we must trust God that it is in our best interests. I have often found encouragement in knowing that when God takes away, it is only to give something better. "They who sow in tears shall reap in joy" (Ps. 126:5). We must believe that God has control of things when someone we really love drops us; the only alternative to this belief is despair.

The great gospel singer, Andrae Crouch, provides an example of how to trust God through great hurts and trials. In his book, *Through It All,* he shares that a bad breakup with a girl he deeply loved caused him to write perhaps his greatest song, "Through it All."

I've had many tears and sorrows,
I've had questions for tomorrow,
There have been times I didn't know right from
      wrong.
But in every situation,
God gave blessed consolation,
That my trials come only to make me strong.

Through it all, through it all,
Oh, I've learned to trust in Jesus,
I've learned to trust in God.
Through it all, through it all,
I've learned to depend upon His Word.

I've been to lots of places,
And I've seen a lot of faces,
There have been times I felt so all alone.
But in my lonely hours,
Yes, those precious lonely hours,
Jesus let me know that I was His own.

I thank God for the mountains,
And I thank Him for the valleys.
I thank Him for the storms He has brought me
    through.
For if I'd never had a problem,
I would never know that He could solve them:
I'd never know what faith in God could do.[1]

Like Andrae Crouch, we too will experience deep hurts. But if we respond as he did, then our problems will but point us to Christ and we will find that Christ is sufficient to meet our every need.

Some time ago I ran across an excellent poem by the famous Christian poet, Christina Rossetti, who had experienced a similar hurt. In her poem she reveals that hurt and rejection by a man she loved caused her to turn to the Lord, where she found complete comfort and utter acceptance.

Twice

I took my heart in my hand
    (O my love, O my love),
I said: Let me fall or stand,
    Let me live or die,

1. Andrae Crouch and Nina Ball, *Through It All* (Waco, Tx: Word, 1974), pp. 93–95.

But this once hear me speak
   (O my love, O my love)
Yet a woman's words are weak;
   You should speak, not I.

You took my heart in your hand
   With a friendly smile,
With a critical eye you scanned,
   Then set it down,
And said: It is still unripe,
   Better wait awhile:
Wait while the skylarks pipe,
   Till the corn grows brown.

As you set it down it broke—
   Broke, but I did not wince,
I smiled at the speech you spoke,
   At your judgment that I heard;
But I have not often smiled
   Since then, nor questioned since,
Nor cared for corn-flowers wild,
   Nor sung with the singing bird.

I take my heart in my hand,
   (O my God, O my God)
My broken heart in my hand,
   Thou hast seen, judge Thou.
My hope was written on sand,
   O my God, O my God:
Now let thy judgment stand—
   Yea, judge me now.

This condemned of a man
   This marred one heedless day,
This heart take thou to scan
   Both within and without:

Refine with fire its gold,
   Purge Thou its dross away—
Yea, hold it in Thy hold,
   Whence none can pluck it out.

I take my heart in my hand—
   I shall not die, but live—
Before they face I stand;
   I, for Thou callest such;
All that I have I bring,
   All that I am I give,
Smile Thou and I shall sing,
   But shall not question much.[2]

Christina Rossetti, like Andrae Crouch, also had learned the secret of finding strength from the Lord during times of great hurt.

Practical Suggestions

After you have resolved between you and the Lord to accept the breakup and to trust the Lord to give you comfort, there are a few things that you can do to help you cope with the situation.

Talk It Over with a Friend

Usually it is best to talk to someone about how you are feeling. Often the sympathy and advice of a friend will help, and you may gain a valuable prayer partner during the hard times ahead.

2. Christina Rossetti, "Twice," in *The Viking Book of Poetry of the English-Speaking World,* ed. Richard Aldington (New York: The Viking Press, 1958), p. 999.

Beware of New Relationships

I think it is important that you begin to date other people again, but beware of immediately getting involved in a new serious relationship. A common response when we are hurt is to immediately seek a new relationship in order to reassure ourselves that we are still attractive to the opposite sex. The problem is, however, that we are usually not emotionally ready for a new relationship. Take some time and get your emotions back under control and settled before you plunge into a new serious relationship.

Avoid Seeing the Old Boy friend/Girlfriend Too Much

Don't see the person who broke up with you any more than necessary. Every time you see them, it may open old wounds. When you are around them, however, be sure to be kind and courteous. Don't give them the "ignore" treatment.

Stay Busy

Don't just sit at home all alone watching TV and listening to depressing music. Get out and do things. Get involved in new things now that you have some additional time. Renew old friendships that you have neglected.

Conclusion

There are going to be times when you will be hurt badly by a breakup. You can count on it! Right now, however, learn to turn to God and to trust Him with the little hurts. You'll find then that you'll be able to turn to Him naturally with the big hurts also. Learn how to "cast all your cares on Him" when problems and hurts come into your life. He is able to heal the brokenhearted and to mend the wounds of love. He will never leave us and is always there when we need Him the most. That's a great comfort when one you love rejects you and your whole world comes crashing down around you. "Even though I walk through the valley of the shadow of death, I fear no evil; for Thou art with me; Thy rod and Thy staff, they comfort me" (Ps. 23:4).

Discussion Questions

Study each passage below and answer the following: What is the purpose of problems in our lives? What should be our response to problems when they come?

1. II Cor. 1:8–10
2. Heb. 12:5–13
3. II Cor. 12:1–10
4. I Peter 4:12, 13
5. John 9:1–7
6. Rom 5:3–5
7. II Cor. 4:6–18
8. II Cor. 1:3–6
9. James 1:2–4
10. Phil. 1:12–14

12

How to Pick a Miss or Mister Without a Mistake

Mrs. Billy Graham once told an audience, "God has not always answered my prayers. If He had, I would have married the wrong man . . . several times." This raises the question, How can you know who God wants you to marry? This is part of the broad, often-asked question, How can I know the will of God? Whole books have been written on this subject, so I won't pretend to cover the whole subject in one short chapter. But I do think some things need to be said about discerning God's will in a life-mate.

Discerning the Will of God: Some Pitfalls

Some people have a distorted notion concerning the method of divine guidance. J. I. Packer, in his outstanding book, *Knowing God,* notes that "their basic mistake is to think of guidance as essentially inward prompting by the Holy Spirit, apart from the written Word."[1] These people rely on an "inward voice" of the Spirit to guide and direct them. They use Romans 8:14 to justify being "led of the Spirit" in this manner.

This method of discerning divine guidance has some serious problems, however. First, "being led of the Spirit" in the context of Romans 8:14 does not relate to "inner voices" but to putting aside known sin in one's life. Being "led of the Spirit" means that I obey God's Word as revealed in the Bible. The method of guidance that depends on receiving inward impressions and leadings by the Spirit is clearly unbiblical. Church history shows that people have used this method to justify terrible false doctrines that are totally contrary to Scripture. Packer writes that "the Spirit leads within the limits which the Word sets, not beyond them."[2]

Another danger in this method of divine guidance is that it is very easy to mistake our wishes for God's will. We mistake our inward desires for the Spirit's leading. It is amazing how easy it is to rationalize the things that we really want. This is especially true in dating relationships. I have heard of people who claimed that God had told them to marry a certain non-Christian. But the Bible clearly instructs us not to marry non-Christians (II Cor. 6:14). I have also heard of young people who said that they felt that it was God's will that they sleep together before they were

1. J. I. Packer, *Knowing God,* p. 212.
2. J. I. Packer, *Knowing God,* p. 215.

married. But the Bible says that "this is the will of God . . . that you abstain from sexual immorality" (I Thess. 4:3). Does God's Spirit lead contrary to God's Word? Never.

It is very clear, then, that we can easily mistake our wishes for His will. When I was dating I began to recognize this difficulty in discerning the will of God in a life-mate. Finally, I discovered that things worked best when I just honestly admitted my wishes and emotions to God and simply prayed, "Lord, you know that I really like this girl. I think that she might be the right one for me. I'm going to pursue this relationship and if she isn't the one that you have for me then *you* shut the door and break apart the relationship or don't let it get started." Though it was often very painful, God was always faithful to answer that prayer.

There was another lesson that I learned when this happened. Since I had prayed that God would shut the door if the relationship was wrong, then I had to be willing to accept it when God shut the door. If God bolted the door, I couldn't run around the house and try to climb in the back window.

Prerequisites to Knowing God's Will

Basically, the key to knowing God's will is, simply, *total commitment to God.* In Romans 12:1, 2, Paul writes,

> I urge you therefore, brethren, by the mercies of God, to present your bodies a living and holy

sacrifice, acceptable to God, which is your spiritual service of worship. And do not be conformed to this world, but be transformed by the renewing of your mind, that you may prove what the will of God is, that which is good and acceptable and perfect.

In Proverbs 3:5, 6 we read:

Trust in the Lord with all your heart,
And do not lean on your own understanding.
In all your ways acknowledge Him,
And He will make your paths straight.

Don't misunderstand me when I say "total commitment." I don't mean that we must be perfect. But I do mean that there must be a basic, sincere, genuine heart desire to please the Lord in our lives. It doesn't mean that we never sin. It doesn't mean that we never slip and fall. But it does mean that the Lord is truly the most important thing in our lives.

Involved in total commitment is a sincere, genuine desire to please and obey God. It is my conviction that we should not concentrate so much on *finding* God's will as on *being in* God's will. God's ultimate will for us is that we might be conformed to the image of Jesus Christ (Rom. 8:29). Therefore, we should not concentrate so much on *finding* the right person as on *being* the right person. God doesn't want us out beating the bushes and prowling for that "right one." Instead, He wants us to concentrate on being and becoming the right person—developing godly character. You see, we tend to attract the sort of people that we are ourselves. And so, if you want a godly mate, then you should concentrate on being a godly person yourself. If you focus on developing godly character in your life, then you can confidently trust God to do His part in bringing the right one to you. Jesus said, "Seek ye first the Kingdom of God, and his righteousness; and all these things shall be added unto you" (Matt. 6:33, KJV).

Along with total commitment, there is one more prerequisite to knowing God's will. It is that we must be *willing to wait*. David learned this secret. In Psalm 37:3–7, he writes,

> Trust in the Lord, and do good;
> Dwell in the land and cultivate faithfulness.
> Delight yourself in the Lord;
> And He will give you the desires of your heart.
> Commit your way to the Lord,
> Trust also in Him, and He will do it. . . .
> Rest in the Lord and wait patiently for Him.

Paul also speaks of this in Phillippians 4:5–7 when he writes,

> Let your forbearing spirit be known to all men. The Lord is near. Be anxious for nothing, but in everything by prayer and supplication with thanksgiving let your requests be made known to God. And the peace of God, which surpasses all comprehension, shall guard your hearts and your minds in Christ Jesus.

Many people think that the worst thing that could happen to them would be to be twenty-five and unmarried. But there is one thing even worse and that is to be twenty-five and married to the wrong person. James Dobson notes that the "threat of being an 'old maid' causes many girls to grab the first train that rambles down the marital track. And too often, it offers a one-way ticket to disaster."[3]

Don't hurry it. Be willing to wait on God's timing. I know it is hard and I know the pressure is difficult, but you will be glad you waited.

How To Know God's Will

First, we need to realize that God *does* have a specific will and plan for our lives. Not only that, but He promises to reveal that plan to us and to guide us.

> I will instruct you and teach you in the way which
> you should go;
> I will counsel you with My eye upon you (Ps. 32:8).

> The Lord will continually guide you,
> And satisfy your desire in scorched places,
> And give strength to your bones;
> And you will be like a watered garden,
> And like a spring of water whose waters do not fail
> (Isa. 58:11).

> Who is the man who fears the Lord?
> He will instruct him in the way he should choose
> (Ps. 25:12).

3. James Dobson, *What Wives Wish Their Husbands Knew About Women*, p. 96.

But if any of you lacks wisdom, let him ask of God,
who gives to all men generously and without
    reproach,
And it will be given to him (James 1:5).[4]

Much of God's will is clearly revealed in the Bible. David writes, "Thy Word is a lamp unto my feet and light unto my path" (Ps. 119:105). For example, Ephesians 5:18 clearly tells us that it is God's will that we be filled with the Spirit. We don't have to ask Him whether or not it is His will that we be filled with the Spirit. He has already told us that it *is* His will. In I Thessalonians 4:3, God tells us that it is His will that we have a morally pure sex life. We don't have to question this. He has already told us what His will is.

The best way to know God's will is to come to know God's Book. Unless we master the Bible, we can never know God's clearly revealed will. The better you know the Bible, the better you will be able to discover God's will. The price tag of knowing God's will is diligent Bible study.

But what about those gray areas where no clear Bible commands are given? Those are the decisions that give us trouble. Should you be a doctor or a lawyer? Should you marry Betty or Debbie? Should you go to the state university or to Bible college? These are the situations where we have the most difficult time discerning God's will.

4. J. I. Packer notes that "wisdom" in Scripture always means knowledge of the course of action that will please God and secure life. *Knowing God*, p. 211.

I don't have any pat answers to this problem, but I do think I have some practical suggestions. First, pray about the decision and then search the Bible looking for principles that might apply to your situation. In Psalm 32:8 God says, "I will instruct you and teach you in the way which you should go: I will counsel you with My eye upon you." But before God will turn His eyes upon us, we need to turn our eyes toward Him and His Word.

Second, examine all sides of the issue. Study the facts. Use your head! Consider the long-term consequences of your decision. List the advantages and disadvantages of each side of the issue.

Third, seek counsel. I was faced with a big decision about where to go to college and God used the counsel of my parents to give me some guidance. Time has shown their advice to have been correct. Proverbs 12:15 tells us that, "The way of a fool is right in his own eyes, but a wise man is he who listens to counsel."

Finally, after you have done all of the above, then *do what seems best to you.* Let me repeat: *Do what seems best to you.* I believe that God uses a believer's common sense. J. I. Packer says that "the fundamental mode whereby our rational Creator guides His rational creatures is by rational understanding and application of His written word."[5] If God is in control of your life, and you have prayed about the decision, and you have sought God's will

5. Packer, *Knowing God,* p. 214.

in Scripture, and you have sought counsel, then it is my conviction that the decision that you make will be God's decision.

If, however, for some reason the decision you make is wrong, I believe that God will somehow stop you. Besides, we need to realize that sometimes decisions that seem wrong to us are right to God. And just because problems and conflicts accompany your decision does not mean that you made the wrong choice. Problems and conflicts often accompany God's will. Paul followed God's guidance and yet faced unbelievable trouble and persecution every step of the way.

Be willing to leave room for God to intervene supernaturally, but don't seek the supernatural. God usually works by natural means, but let us not be guilty of boxing God in and saying that He always has to work in such and such a way.

Is God's Will Worth Waiting For?

Some people feel that if they trust God for a mate then He will give them the dullest, ugliest person alive! This is utterly false. Romans 12:2 says that God's will is good, acceptable, and perfect. We are God's children. He is our heavenly Father. He loves us and is committed to meeting all our needs. In Matthew 7:9-11, Jesus says,

> Or what man is there among you, when his son shall ask him for a loaf, will give him a stone? Or if he shall ask for a fish, he will not give him a snake,

will he? If you then, being evil, know how to give good gifts to your children, how much more shall your Father who is in heaven give what is good to those who ask Him!

I know that you get impatient and that you sometimes feel God has forgotten you. But from the authority of the Word of God you can know that God has not forgotten you and that He promises to provide for your every need. Listen very closely. *God is far more concerned about a partner for your life than you could ever be—even in your most down and depressed moments!* Let me repeat that. God is far more concerned about a partner in your life than you could ever be—even in your most down and depressed moments. God is looking out for you. He is your Father. He loves you and He promises to give you the very best. Wait on Him and He will give you the desires of your heart.

Is There Only One "Right One" for Me?

There is one more question that we need to deal with under this topic of knowing God's will for a mate. Some people teach that God has only one special person for you and that you will never have a maximum marriage unless you discover and marry that one special person. There is one serious problem with this view, however. If either of you make a wrong choice and instead marry someone else, then both of you are doomed to an unhappy life and a less than maximum marriage.

I had to struggle with this problem while in college. I fell in love with a girl and was convinced that she was the "right one." For four long years I prayed diligently that God would give her to me as my wife, but she married another man. Either I was wrong or I am doomed to have a less-than-maximum marriage with my wife, because this other girl was not listening to the Lord. I prefer to think that I was wrong. There are perhaps thousands of people that you could marry and be happy with. The person you marry becomes God's will for you as long as the marriage does not violate any of the biblical principles given concerning marriage such as marrying a non-Christian.

Choosing a life-mate is a *very big* decision. It is a decision that should not be made without much prayer and soul-searching. But if we will follow the principles in this chapter, I believe that God will give us special wisdom and guidance.

Discussion Questions

1. What should you do if you must make a decision and there are no clear commands or principles in Scripture that apply to your situation?

2. Look up *will* in your Bible concordance. What are three things that Scripture says are definitely God's will?

3. Study Genesis 24 carefully. What principles can you discover concerning how to know whom to marry? Do you think God operates this way today?

4. Study I Corinthians 16:8, 9 and Acts 16:6, 7. What do these passages teach about the will of God?

5. In Proverbs 3:5, 6, God says that He will make our paths straight (that is, show us His will) if we do three things. What are these three things and what do they mean?

6. Would there ever be an instance where God's Spirit might lead contrary to God's Word?

13

To Wed or Not to Wed?

Before we conclude this discussion of knowing God's will for a mate, perhaps we had better ask if it is God's will for you to marry at all. You see, there are two basic states—marriage and singleness. Often, we are indirectly taught that marriage is the only option for the spiritual Christian. Those who are unmarried are merely waiting to meet the "right one." In his booklet, "A Single Person's Identity," John Fisher remarks that single people are made to feel they are like an airplane in a "holding pattern," flying around trying to find the airport so that they can land, that is, get married and then *really* start living. This pressure is not too strong when you are young and still in high school, but it will get stronger and stronger the older you get. Often single people are made to feel like second-rate citizens, "incomplete" because they are not married. They are always being encouraged to look toward the future, to the time when they marry.[1]

This attitude, though, is clearly unbiblical. The Bible has many positive things to say about singleness. As a matter of fact, the New Testament has almost as much to say about singleness as it does about marriage! The two key passages on the subject are I Corinthians 7 and Matthew 19:1–12. The passages are very similar, and we will focus our attention in this chapter on I Corinthians.

The Gift of Singleness

Both Paul and Matthew teach that singleness is a gift from God. You may be thinking, "That's the kind of gift that I can do without!" But the Bible teaches that this gift is something good. Paul had this special gift and says that it is something to be desired.

The Purpose of the Gift

We have already seen in Genesis 2:18 that God's norm is that we marry. The *general principle* is that it is not good for man to be alone. But there are *certain cases* where God says that it is good for man to be alone. When God gives a special gift of singleness, it is good for man to be alone, and it is for a very good reason.

1. John Fisher, "*A Single Person's Identity*", p. 1.

I Corinthians 7:25–35 tells us that the purpose of the gift of singleness is to free a person for *undistracted devotion to the Lord.* When one is married, he is responsible both to his mate and to the Lord. He has a responsibility to serve both, and so his interests are divided. This is inevitable and necessary, and the way married life should be. An unmarried person, however, can serve the Lord without distractions. He can keep whatever hours he wishes and not have the responsibility of a family. He has the advantage of *freedom.* He can come and go and serve without distraction.

This does not mean that the married person is any less spiritual or loves the Lord less. But common sense tells us that he cannot do as much for the Lord because his time is limited. Thus, the difference is *service, not spirituality.*

The Lord Is Coming Soon

In I Corinthians 7:29 and 31, Paul tells us why undistracted devotion is so important. It is important because "the time has been shortened" (v. 29) and "this world is passing away" (v. 31). There is an urgency in this life. The Lord is coming soon and the time to work is getting shorter and shorter. Paul says in Romans 13:11, 12 that "salvation is nearer to us than when we [first] believed. The night is almost gone, and the day is at hand." Jesus said in John 9:4, "We must work the works of Him who sent Me, as long as it is day; night is coming, when no man can work."

How Can I Know If I Have the Gift?

I have met many enthusiastic young Christians who once vowed that they would never marry but would remain a "celibate for Christ" or a "bachelor till the rapture!" But, as the years passed, this zeal slowly died and they married. Why did this happen?

Obviously, they desired the gift and yet did not have it. The gift of singleness is a special God-given ability to control one's sexual desires and to be content without being married. Most people simply can't do this. Though God gives us grace to control our sexual desires while we are single, it is a great struggle and rarely can we say that we are fully content in the single state. Most of us have certain needs and desires that can be fulfilled only by a marriage relationship. When God gives the gift of singleness, however, He fulfills these needs.

I have met some people who are very content being single. Sure, sometimes they are lonely and sometimes they desire sexual expression, but on the whole, they are happy as singles. These people have the gift of singleness and should not actively pursue marriage unless God changes their desires.

On the other hand, there are those who have a strong desire for a marriage relationship. They are clearly discontented in the single state. Their devotion to the Lord is more distracted by their problems with self-control and discontentment than they would be with a husband or wife. They probably don't have the gift and should start praying toward marriage. In

I Timothy 5:14, Paul tells young women who have strong sensual desires to get married.

The Gift Can Be Temporary

It is my conviction that the gift of singleness can be temporary. The gift of singleness does not necessarily imply that one remains forever in that state. God can call a man to singleness and then call him to marriage.

I have heard many godly saints, who are now married, share that for years they were completely content being single. Then God brought a restlessness and discontentment into their lives which was satisfied only with a mate. Many Old Testament saints were relatively old when they married. Isaac was forty years old when he married (Gen. 25:20), and Moses was over forty (Exod. 2:21). Surely God gave these great men a contentment without being married.

Single Living in a Married World

As a young single, there is sometimes a great deal of pressure to marry early. But Paul in I Corinthians 7 says that there should be no hurry to marry. Give the Lord all your undistracted devotion in your youth for as long as you can.

Maybe the best policy is to simply focus on living for the Lord one day at a time and not to worry about whether or not God has a mate for you. James warns us about making too many plans for the future without considering the Lord (James 4:13).

Don't Give Up Dating!

If you think that you might have this gift or might want to try to cultivate it, don't misunderstand me—I'm not saying that you should give up dating. As we have already seen in chapter 1, dating has many other purposes besides finding a wife or a husband. Just because you may have the gift does not mean that you should give up all of your relationships with the opposite sex. For even if you have the gift, you still have certain social needs. Dating is very important no matter what your gift may be.

Discussion Questions

1. Read I Corinthians 7:1–9. What is Paul saying about marriage in vv. 7–9?

2. What gift is Paul referring to in I Corinthians 7:7?

3. Read I Corinthians 7:25–35. Why does Paul say that it is better for a person to remain single?

4. Read Matthew 19:1–12. What is the statement that Jesus says not all men can accept in v. 11?

5. In Matthew 19:11, Jesus says that only those "to whom it has been given" can accept this statement. What has been given?

6. What are the three types of eunuchs in Matthew 19:12?

7. Is it wrong to marry? Why, or why not?

14

Engagement
and Marriage

A couple should not only consider the question of
God's will in choosing a mate (though that is primary), but should also weigh several other factors
before becoming engaged. Statistics show that 72
percent of American women who marry between 14
and 17 will eventually get divorced. 46 percent of
those who marry at 18 or 19 will get divorced.[1] Before
you consider marriage, you should ask yourself
some hard questions.

1. Population Reference Bureau.

Considering Marriage

Are You Willing To Live with this Person, Even If He or She Never Changes?

Kathy was deeply in love with Sam. They had met five months earlier and had really hit it off—well, almost. Kathy was a Christian and Sam was not. This bothered Kathy sometimes but she was sure that Sam would change and become a Christian after they married. Sam also had some other faults— every now and then Sam would really blow his top. But Kathy was in love and she thought that her love would change these things in Sam once they married. They were married in June. The next March the divorce was final! What happened? Well, Sam didn't change after all. As a matter of fact, he got worse.

The story is common. Time after time couples go into marriage ignoring serious areas of difficulty and expecting each other to change after the wedding. We need to recognize, however, that marriage *may* change a person, but the odds are against it. You are still the same person after you are married that you were before marriage. In fact, marriage often magnifies and increases problem areas because the two of you are now forced to live so close together. Marriage reveals what you are on the inside.

Perhaps the best policy is not to expect to change your mate after you marry. Then, if he (or she) doesn't change, you won't be disappointed. But on the other hand, if your mate does change, you can be pleasantly surprised! The question that you need to face, then, is, "Would I be willing to live with this person even if he never changed?" Are you willing to accept and love him unconditionally the way he is, without demanding that he change?

Do You Generally Get Along Well?

Do you find that you are best friends? Do you *like* one another? Sure, you say, "We *love* one another!" That is not what I am asking. Do you *like* one another? All through the Song of Solomon we see that Solomon and his wife were best friends as well as lovers (Song of Sol. 5:16). Do you get along well or do you find that you have frequent disagreements and arguments? Can you just sit down with one another and talk easily? If you have problems in any of these areas, then I would suggest that you wait a while and see if you can work some of these things out before you become engaged.

Why Do You Want to Get Married?

People get married for many different reasons. Some reasons are good and some are bad. What are some of the bad reasons for getting married?

Your Friends Are All Doing It

Young people are greatly influenced by the actions of their friends. Often one couple may get engaged and so the others get on the roller coaster and also get engaged.

To Escape

A young person may sometimes marry simply to escape the pressures of home or school or work. Sometimes a person may be unhappy in his or her present situation and marriage looks like a way of escape. Needless to say, this sort of marriage has a very weak foundation.

Marriage on the Rebound

Sometimes after a person has been hurt, he looks to marry the first person who comes along. He so desperately needs love and assurance that he grabs the first person that comes along without looking at things rationally and logically.

Sexual Attraction Alone

Many times two young people marry solely on the basis of sexual attraction. They marry a body rather than a person. Unfortunately, the specialness of sex may quickly wear off in marriage when there is no deep commitment. If there is not a strong relationship in addition to sex then there is little to hold the two together after the honeymoon.

Pregnancy

It has been estimated that out of every ten teenagers who get pregnant, three are married, three get married, and four either have abortions or have their babies without getting married.[2] Other statistics

2. Theodore Litz, *The Person*, p. 367.

show that a large percentage of brides are pregnant when they marry. If you find yourself pregnant and unmarried, there are several options open to you. Your options are (1) to get married, (2) to keep the child and remain unmarried, or (3) to put the child up for adoption and remain unmarried. I did not mention abortion as an option because I believe that the Bible teaches that abortion is murder (Ps. 139:13; Jer. 1:5; Ps. 51:5.) If you find yourself pregnant and unmarried, perhaps the best advice that I can give to you is to seek the advice of your pastor, a qualified Christian counselor, or a Christian psychiatrist.

Some good reasons for wanting to get married include genuine love, the desire for companionship, the desire for a family, and the desire for sexual expression.

How Will Your Parents Respond to Your Marriage?

When you get married, you are not only marrying a person but you are also marrying a family. If either set of parents is against the marriage, you will probably have in-law conflicts and may lose their much-needed support and advice. Many times your parents can see problems in the marriage that you can't predict because they have gone through it all. Beware of rejecting the advice of your parents.

Can You Handle It Financially?

Many couples in love ignore the financial side of marriage and think that they can "live on love." But financial problems are a major cause for divorce.

There are many, many expenses related to a wedding, setting up a home, and supporting a family that couples often don't consider.

Frequently when a couple marries early, the guy is forced to drop out of school and go to work. His inexperience forces him to take poor jobs. The poor paying job forces him to work long hours, which puts a strain on the young marriage relationship. The couple is always tired and has neither the time nor the money for a social life outside of the home. The long hours and poor pay prevents the guy from going back to school. If a child comes along at this time, there are even more financial burdens, and the wife is kept from working. Also, a new child, apart from the financial burden, places certain stresses on a marriage.

Because of all of this, perhaps the advice of Benjamin Franklin is worth following. He said, "First thrive, then wive."

Are You Looking for the Perfect Mate?

This is often a problem. A girl may have a picture in the back of her mind of the Prince Charming that she expects to marry. Many people make up long lists of qualities that their mate *must* have. When they begin to date a person, out comes the list. When the person doesn't measure up to the list, they move on to someone else, always looking for that perfect mate. If this describes you, then prepare yourself. I have something very important to tell you. You will *never* find the perfect mate! The reason for this is that nobody is perfect. Sure, you should have an idea of what you want in a mate, but be willing to bend at certain points.

Don't Settle for Second Best

Don't marry someone that you can just live with. Instead, marry someone that you can't live without!

Engagement

Engagement is a transition period between dating and marriage. It is the time when you have committed yourselves to one another to become husband and wife. The question is no longer "if," but "when." Engagement is a solemn step to be taken only after much prayer and consideration of the eight principles that we have just shared. It should never be taken if there is still any question in your mind whether or not you will marry this person. When you become engaged, you are saying, "I am willing to marry you *right now*." The decision has been made and is final in your mind. *Never* get engaged if you have the slightest thought that you might break off the engagement later on. Sure, there will be times when engagements will have to be broken off, but try to settle the questions in your mind *before* you get engaged, not *after*.

Purposes of the Engagement Period

Engagement should primarily be a time for making mutual plans for the future, preparing yourselves for married life, and planning the wedding. There are many things that you must plan and talk out during the engagement period.

Wedding Plans

Planning a wedding is more work than you might think. Talk to friends, your minister, or a bridal consultant well before the big day.

Finances

Have you thought about how much money it will take to get married, to set up housekeeping, and then to live on? How do you both feel about the wife working? Have you set up a budget? Have you checked into insurance? These things and many more need to be carefully thought out.

Preparing for Sex

Don't assume that you already know everything about sex. Take a crash reading course *just before the wedding.* I would recommend that you read several books:

Tim LaHaye, *The Act of Marriage,* (Grand Rapids: Zondervan, 1977.)
Herbert Miles, *Sexual Happiness in Marriage,* (Grand Rapids: Zondervan, 1970.)
Joseph Dillow, *Solomon on Sex,* (Nashville: Thomas Nelson Publishers, 1977.)

Also there are some excellent tapes by Ed Wheat, a Christian family physician, titled "Sex Techniques and Sex Problems in Marriage." You can obtain these from Bible Believers Cassettes, Inc., 130 Spring, Springdale, Arizona, 72764.

Attitudes toward Children

What are your views toward children? Do you want children? Do you agree on how to raise children? Educate yourselves in this area. I would recommend Paul Meier's *Christian Child-Rearing and Personality Development,* and Howard G. Hendricks's *Heaven Help the Home!*

In-laws

One of the most common sources of marital friction is in-law problems. You need to cultivate your in-laws' support and friendship. Your mate belonged to them first. Don't assume them to be outlaws just because they are in-laws. They can be your best friends in marriage.

Premarital Counseling

I would highly recommend that you undergo several premarital marriage counseling sessions. This was one of the most helpful things I did to prepare for marriage. Usually your pastor, a trained Christian marriage counselor, or a Christian psychiatrist can counsel you. This may perhaps be the best help you can get in making the important early adjustments to married life.

Finally, perhaps the best book to read while you are engaged is *Getting Ready for Marriage,* by David Mace.

Marriage

The Divine Institution of Marriage (Genesis 2:24)

Marriage is one of the greatest gifts that God ever gave to man. In the Garden of Eden, God saw that it was not good for man to be alone. And so He created woman, brought her to the man, and instituted the marriage relationship. Marriage is divinely ordained and created by God. Paul tells us in Hebrews that it is to be "held in honor by all" (Heb. 13:4). In Matthew 19:4-6, Jesus endorsed it as a divine institution and in John 2, He blessed marriage by His presence at the wedding of Cana.

In Genesis 2:24, we see that there are three things that form a marriage.

"A Man Shall Leave His Father and Mother."

A man and a woman are to leave their respective parents and are to form a new home. One relationship must be broken before another relationship can be established. Out of this new relationship and new home will grow a new family. Both the man and woman need to make a clean break with their former homes.

". . . And Shall Cleave to His Wife."

This speaks of commitment. Both promise and covenant to love, honor, and serve one another in poverty as in wealth, in sickness as in health, and in joy as in sorrow, as long as they both shall live. The ring given is the token of this everlasting commitment of love. There is no such thing as marriage in the eyes of God apart from this commitment.

". . . And They Shall Become One Flesh."

This speaks of sexual union. Sex is a gift given by God to us. Sex in the marriage relationship is good and right and is to be enjoyed (Song of Sol., Prov. 5:18, 19).

The Divine Regulations Concerning Marriage

There are several important regulations concerning marriage that are found in Scripture.

Marriage Must Be "in the Lord" Only

This means that it is wrong for a believer to marry an unbeliever (I Cor. 7:39; 9:5; II Cor. 6:14, 15.)

Marriage Is To Be Permanent

God's design is one man for one woman—for life! Only death legitimately breaks the marriage bond (Matt. 5:32; Mark 10:9; Rom. 7:2).

This of course raises the question of divorce. There is much division on this subject because there is some difficulty in interpreting some of the Bible passages relating to it. It may be that the Bible permits divorce on the basis of adultery (Matt. 19:3-9) or desertion by the unbelieving mate (I Cor. 7:10), but divorce is *never* endorsed and *never* encouraged by God (Matt. 19:3-9; Mal. 2:16). Don't dare go into marriage thinking that you can get a divorce if it doesn't work out! Of course, there will be problems in your marriage, but make your mind up before you are married that you will labor to work out your problems instead of dropping the relationship and running.

Marriage Partners Have Mutual Responsibilities

All through the Bible we see that God has ordained different roles and responsibilities for men and women. Wives are to submit to their husbands (Eph. 5:22). This is not a popular doctrine today, but it is clearly taught in Scripture. It is found also in I Corinthians 11:2, Genesis 3:16, I Peter 3:1, Titus 2:5, and I Timothy 2:9-15. The man is to be the head in the marriage relationship and the woman is to be subject to her husband's leadership.

This does not mean, though, that the woman is inferior to the man or that the husband is to be a dictator. It does not even mean that the husband is always right! But it does mean that the man has the final word in decisions, after thorough discussion and prayer with his wife.

Husbands are to love their wives (Eph. 5:25). The husband is to love his wife the way Christ loves the church. Christ sacrificed His own life for the church, and the husband should have the same attitude toward his wife. This is a very sober and challenging responsibility. So often Christians stress that the woman is to submit and yet ignore this equally vital responsibility of the husband. Both roles and responsibilities are vital to a successful marriage.

Marriage is an exciting thing to look forward to. It is my prayer that God has used this book to better prepare you for marriage through your dating life.

Why don't you bow your head right now and ask God to prepare you and your mate-to-be for your future marriage? Then ask Him to give you the power through His Holy Spirit to practice the biblical principles of dating that you have learned in this book.

Discussion Questions

1. Read Ephesians 5:22–33. Which verses are addressed to wives and which are addressed to husbands?
2. What is the primary responsibility of the wife?
3. What is the primary responsibility of the husband?
4. In vv. 23 and 24, how does Paul illustrate the responsibility of the wife to submit?
5. What does it mean to "be subject to your own husband"?
6. In vv. 25–27, how does Paul illustrate the way that husbands ought to love their wives?
7. What is another illustration that Paul uses to show how the husband ought to love his wife? (vv. 28, 29).
8. What is the relationship of v. 33 to the preceding verses?
9. What do you think this passage has to say in relation to the "women's lib" movement?
10. Does this passage teach that women are inferior because they must submit to their husbands? Why, or why not?
11. Does this pasage teach that husbands are to be dictators? Why, or why not?

Bibliography

Books

Clemens, David A. "The Believer and the Opposite Sex." *The Cutting Edge* (vol. 2 of *Steps to Maturity*), Bible Club Movement, Inc.

Duvall, Evelyn M. and Johnson, Joy D. *The Art of Dating.* Rev. ed. New York: Association Press, 1967.

Evening, Margaret. *Who Walk Alone.* Downers Grove, Ill.: InterVarsity Press, 1974.

Fisher, John. *A Single Person's Identity.* Palo Alto, Calif.: Discovery Publishing, 1973.

Hartley, Fred. *Update.* Old Tappan, N. J.: Revell, 1977.

Hendricks, Howard G. *Heaven Help the Home!* Wheaton, Ill.: Victor Books, 1973.

Householder, William Joel, "Sex and the Single High School Student." Unpublished master's thesis, Dallas Theological Seminary, 1975.

Mace, David. *Getting Ready for Marriage.* Nashville: Abingdon, 1972.

McAllister, Dawson. *Discussion Manual for Student Relationships.* Glendale, Calif.: Shepherd Productions, 1975.

McGinnis, Marilyn. *Single: The Woman's View.* Old Tappan, N. J.: Revell, 1974.

Meier, Paul D. *Christian Child-Rearing and Personality Development.* Grand Rapids: Baker, 1977.

Miles, Herbert J. *The Dating Game.* Grand Rapids: Zondervan, 1975.

Olford, Stephen F., and Lawes, Frank A. *The Sanctity of Sex.* Old Tappan, N. J.: Revell, n.d.

Osborne, Cecil. *The Art of Understanding Your Mate.* Grand Rapids: Zondervan, 1970.

Rice, Max, and Rice, Vivian. *When Can I Say "I Love You?"* Chicago: Moody Press, 1977.

Richards, Lawrence. *How Far Can I Go?* Chicago: Moody Press, 1969.

Ridenour, Fritz. *The Other Side of Morality.* Glendale, Calif.: Gospel Light Publications, 1969.

Shedd, Charlie W. *Letters to Philip.* Old Tappan, N. J.: Revell, 1969.

Shedd, Charlie W. *Letters to Karen.* Old Tappan, N. J.: Revell, n.d.

Small, Dwight Hervey. *Design for Christian Marriage.* Old Tappan, N. J.: Revell, 1971.

Stafford, Tim. *A Love Story.* Grand Rapids: Zondervan, 1977.

Sweeting, George. *Love Is the Greatest.* Chicago: Moody Press, 1974.

White, John. *Eros Defiled: The Christian and Sexual Sin.* Downers Grove, Ill.: InterVarsity Press, 1977.

Periodicals

Anonymous. "Did I Miss God's Best?" *Christian Life,* June 1971, p. 47.

Florio, Anthony. "Danger Signs for the Not Yet Married." *Psychology for Living,* April 1975, p. 17.

Frost, Heidi. "Who's the Lucky One?" *Faith at Work,* Oct. 1974, p. 9.

Hancock, Maxine. "Samson: Passion's Slave." *HIS,* Nov. 1974, p. 1.

Larson, Bruce. "The Gift of Loneliness." *Faith at Work,* Oct. 1974, p. 26.

Massey, Craig. "The Many Ways of Love." *Moody Monthly,* Oct. 1974, p. 28.

Spanier, Graham B. "Sexualization and Premarital Sexual Behavior." *Family Coordinator,* Jan. 1975, pp. 33–40.

Springer, Joel; Springer, Suzanne; and Aaronson, Barry. "An Approach to Teaching a Course on Dating Behavior." *The Family Coordinator,* Jan. 1975, pp. 13–18.

Tompkins, Charles. "Fellows Only." *Moody Monthly,* May 1972, p. 97.

Wilkinson, Melvin. "Romantic Love: The Great Equalizer? Sexism in Popular Music." *Family Coordinator,* April, 1976.